THE **LITTLE BOOK** OF
BONSAI

The Little Book of Bonsai
Author: Malcolm and Kath Hughes
First published in Great Britain in 2016 by Mitchell Beazley,
an imprint of Octopus Publishing Group Ltd,
Carmelite House, 50 Victoria Embankment, London, EC4Y 0DZ
www.octopusbooks.co.uk   www.octopusbooksusa.com
Distributed in the US by
Hachette Book Group
1290 Avenue of the Americas
4th and 5th Floors
New York, NY 10020

Distributed in Canada by
Canadian Manda Group
664 Annette St.
Toronto, Ontario, Canada M6S 2C8

ISBN: 978 1 78472 170 1

Gill Sans, Rockwell and Quickpen
Printed and bound in China
Mitchell Beazley Publisher: Alison Starling

Conceived, designed and produced by
Quid Publishing
Part of The Quarto Group
Level 4 Sheridan House
Hove BN3 1DD
England
Cover design: Clare Barber
Designer: Clare Barber
Illustrations: Melvyn Evans
Consultant editor: Simon Maughan

THE **LITTLE BOOK** OF
BONSAI

Master the Art of Growing Miniature Trees

MALCOLM & KATH HUGHES

MITCHELL
BEAZLEY

CONTENTS

Chapter 3:

SPECIES PROFILES...88

APPENDIX:

INTRODUCTION

After many centuries of being confined to China and later Japan, there are now few countries in the world where bonsai are not grown. Growing bonsai has become a common bond, bringing people of all nations together in a love of these beautiful small trees. It is a hobby we can all enjoy and we do not need to speak foreign languages to be able to communicate our shared love of bonsai. The beauty of the tree speaks for itself.

Bonsai combines the beauty of man-made sculpture with the harmony and perfection of nature in one art form. All parts of a bonsai—the roots, trunk, branches, foliage, and container—must, like traditional sculpture, express the artist's feeling for balance, form, and line. When these are combined with the forces of the natural world, they can evoke a larger and deeper concept. A bonsai is a miniature representation of the mystery of the universe, unchanged in everything but size.

With associations such as this, it comes as no surprise that there is a certain mystique about bonsai. This oriental obsession for miniature trees would appear to be governed by arcane Japanese secrets. Why else would they be so rare and expensive? This is just one of a plethora of Western myths about bonsai that needs to be shattered.

HOW TO USE THIS BOOK

This book includes everything you could want to know if you wish to grow bonsai—from what they are and the origins of this fascinating art to the different species of trees suitable for creating bonsai, how to obtain them, the equipment and skills you need to keep them healthy, right through to displaying them. With a helpful guide to the art of bonsai, it is a book that can be either dipped into or read from cover to cover, depending on where your interests lie.

Chapter 1:

GETTING STARTED We start by looking at the history of bonsai and its origins in ancient China and Japan, and how bonsai spread throughout the Western world. We also explain how to acquire materials suitable for bonsai, and all the equipment you need to get started. Bonsai tools, pots, soils, wire, and fertilizers are all here, with clear guidance on how best to use them.

Chapter 2:

BONSAI TECHNIQUES AND CARE

This chapter explains in detail the techniques you require to style trees and to keep them healthy. Styling, pruning, wiring, and repotting are all explained, as well as how the care of your bonsai changes through the seasons and what requirements

these trees have in our changing patterns of weather. Also covered are the various problems you may encounter and how best to prevent pests and, if necessary, how to rid yourself of them. The chapter ends with a clearly illustrated guide to the basic bonsai styles.

Chapter 3:

SPECIES PROFILES

A clear guide, with illustrations of the species of trees most suitable for creating bonsai. It is not a definitive guide, because it is possible to use any living tree, but some have better characteristics than others.

Finally, we look at some of the many ways to display your trees, followed by a glossary of terms and a list of useful resources for sourcing bonsai and related products and equipment.

Chapter 1

GETTING STARTED

Bonsai is an enjoyable hobby and form of art. Unlike most other art forms, bonsai is unique in that the canvas is alive and changing. Aside from the art, you require some knowledge of horticulture, because you need to know not only how to make the tree look good but also how to keep it alive. With the right care, bonsai trees can live as long as normal-sized adult trees, if not longer. After all, you are giving them far more care and attention than any tree in the wild receives. Most people seem to start growing bonsai after buying a ready-made bonsai tree. It is without a doubt a good way to get started, but it could prove less expensive if you learn what to look for when choosing your tree and how to keep it alive. Here we plan to give you that information.

WHAT ARE BONSAI?

Bonsai are ordinary living trees that have been miniaturized using specialized techniques. In the process, they are shaped so that they express the beauty of a tree growing in nature.

To watch a maple tree—small enough to hold in your hands—sprout its tiny buds in the spring, fill out with green foliage in the summer, turn bright red or orange in the fall, and drop its leaves in the winter is to experience wonder. Bonsai allow us to take a pause in the relentless pace of daily life, and connect with nature's great calm.

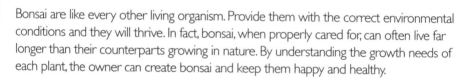

Bonsai are like every other living organism. Provide them with the correct environmental conditions and they will thrive. In fact, bonsai, when properly cared for, can often live far longer than their counterparts growing in nature. By understanding the growth needs of each plant, the owner can create bonsai and keep them happy and healthy.

TREES IN POTS

Bonsai can vary in height from a few inches to several feet. There is no finite height limit—the only constraint is that it must be cultivated in a pot. However, not every tree grown in a pot can be called a bonsai. It must have certain characteristics to qualify for the name. It must be artistic in shape and, of course, miniature in size. It should be a replica in miniature, a small-scale version of a fully grown tree, and it must be in an appropriate pot, not an ice cream carton or a small plastic flower pot. The pot should be part of the pleasing aesthetic appearance.

BONSAI MYTHS

- **Bonsai are special dwarf types of trees.** They are not genetic dwarfs but ordinary examples of their species. True dwarf trees grow so slowly they would take forever to develop.

- **Growing bonsai in pots keeps them small.** In fact, it is regular pruning that keeps them small. Bonsai trees are regularly repotted to keep them growing vigorously. Sometimes they are grown in the ground for a few years to "fatten up" more quickly, then transferred to a pot.

BONSAI COME IN A RANGE OF SHAPES AND SIZES

- **Bonsai are difficult to grow and keep happy.** They are no more difficult to look after than other pot plants, and easier than many.

- **Bonsai are tiny, only a few inches tall.** Actually, they come in a range of sizes from a few inches up to several feet tall.

- **The biggest trees are the oldest and most valuable.** Age is a real red herring with bonsai: a high-quality younger tree made to look old will always win out over a much older but dull one.

- **Bonsai are indoor plants.** When it comes to bonsai, "indoor" is a somewhat misleading term. There is no tree in the world bred to grow indoors. However, there are trees that naturally grow in countries whose climates are similar to the conditions inside our houses—therefore they will happily live indoors.

BONSAI THROUGH THE AGES

Although the word "bonsai" is Japanese, the art it describes originated in China. Even today, the Japanese characters for bonsai remain the same as the Chinese. By the year 700 AD, the Chinese had started the art of "pun-tsai," using these special techniques to grow dwarf trees in shallow containers. It was later adopted by the Japanese, where it developed along slightly different lines due to the influence of Zen Buddhism and the fact that Japan is so much smaller than China and growing space is much more limited. Known only slightly outside Asia for many centuries, it is only relatively recently that bonsai has spread to the rest of the world.

BONSAI IN CHINA

The tomb paintings for Crown Prince Zhang Huaia, dating from about 706 AD, depict ladies-in-waiting offering miniature rockery landscapes with small plants in shallow dishes, suggesting that bonsai existed as early as the eighth century. However, the first mention of bonsai appears on a Japanese scroll painted during the Kamakura period (1192–1333). The scroll itself depicts life during the Heian period (794–1185) and illustrates miniature trees planted in shallow basins or pots.

Japanese scroll painting depicting bonsai being offered for sale (dated between 1780 and 1820).

Shallow porcelain bowls
had been made in what we now call
China for at least 5,000 years. Then
the principal of the Chinese Five Agents (water, fire,
wood, metal, and earth) led to the idea of miniature
replicas of nature. By creating them, albeit on a
reduced scale, it was believed you could gain control
of their mystical properties. This was the start of
miniature landscapes and subsequently miniature trees.

The earliest collected and then containerized trees are believed to have been
peculiarly shaped and twisted specimens from the wild. They were "sacred"—
these trees could not be used for any practical, ordinary purposes. Their strange
forms and shapes were reminiscent of yoga-type postures that repeatedly bent
back on themselves, recirculating vital fluids said to promote long life.

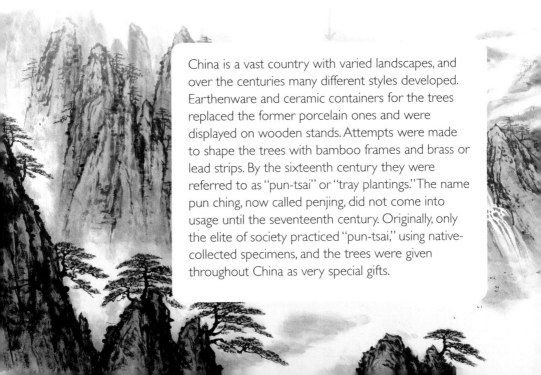

China is a vast country with varied landscapes, and
over the centuries many different styles developed.
Earthenware and ceramic containers for the trees
replaced the former porcelain ones and were
displayed on wooden stands. Attempts were made
to shape the trees with bamboo frames and brass or
lead strips. By the sixteenth century they were
referred to as "pun-tsai" or "tray plantings." The name
pun ching, now called penjing, did not come into
usage until the seventeenth century. Originally, only
the elite of society practiced "pun-tsai," using native-
collected specimens, and the trees were given
throughout China as very special gifts.

BONSAI IN JAPAN

The Japanese were fascinated by all things Chinese, and bonsai was one of many Chinese cultural traditions adopted by the Japanese, along with Chan Buddhism, which became Zen Buddhism in Japan. Bonsai was first adopted by the Japanese during the Kamakura period, but it was during the Edo period (1615–1868) that gardening and small potted trees became most popular in Japan. Finding beauty in severe austerity, Zen monks developed their own tray landscapes along more simple lines so that a single tree in a pot could represent the universe. The Japanese pots were generally deeper than those from China.

Everyone from the shoguns to ordinary peasant people grew some form of tree or plant in a pot. By the late eighteenth century, a show for traditional potted dwarf pine trees was started and held annually in the capital city of Kyoto. Around the year 1800, a group of Japanese students of Chinese art gathered in Osaka to discuss styles of miniature trees. These scholars renamed the trees "bonsai" (the Japanese pronunciation of the Chinese pun-tsai). Bonsai was now seen as a matter of design, the artistic approach replacing the religious-mythical traditional approach. Variations of sizes and styles were developed; catalogues and books about these trees, tools, and pots were published and some early exhibitions were held.

BEECH
(FAGUS SYLVATICA)

Staff member watering a Japanese five-needle pine on display at the Saitama Omiya Bonsai Museum of Art in Japan.

Following the Great Kantō Earthquake that devastated the Tokyo area in 1923, a group of thirty families of professional growers resettled twenty miles away in Omiya and set up what would become the center of Japanese bonsai culture—Omiya Bonsai Village. In the 1930s, formal displays of bonsai became recognized, and an official annual exhibition started at Tokyo's Metropolitan Museum of Art, which still exists today as the Kokufu Exhibition. The end of World War II saw the art of bonsai mature and many were cultivated as an important art form. Apprenticeship programs and great numbers of shows, books, magazines, and classes for foreigners evolved outside Japan. The use of power tools matched with an intricate knowledge of plant physiology allowed a few masters to move from the craft approach to a true horticultural art form.

BONSAI IN THE WEST

In the seventeenth century, a description in Spanish was discovered of Chinese immigrants in the tropical islands of the Philippines growing small ficus trees onto hand-sized pieces of coral. The earliest English observation of potted dwarf trees in China/Macau was recorded in 1637. Dozens of travelers included mention of dwarf trees in their accounts of visits to Japan or China. Japanese dwarf trees were seen in the Philadelphia Exposition in 1876, the Paris Expositions of 1878 and 1889, the Chicago Exposition of 1893, the St Louis World's Fair of 1904, the 1910 Japan-Britain Exhibition, and at the 1915 San Francisco Exposition. The tiny trees were greeted with feelings of astonishment and a sense of awe. However, many who purchased specimens were sorely disappointed when the little trees died. The new owners did not have the knowledge to properly care for them, and their original fascination gave way to the question "How do you keep them alive?".

The first European language book entirely about Japanese dwarf trees was published in 1902, and the first in English in 1940. Yoshimura and Halford's *Miniature Trees and Landscapes* was published in 1957. It would become known as the "Bible of Bonsai in the West," with Yuji Yoshimura being the link between Japanese classical bonsai art and the more progressive Western approach. John Naka, a Japanese American from California, started teaching in California and produced his now-famous books on the art.

Over the years, improvements have been made to the revered old bonsai nurseries in Japan, and these have been brought into the Western world by visiting teachers or returning travelers.

Early European books about bonsai focussed on skills and techniques required for keeping trees alive, as well as explaining the aesthetics involved in styling and shaping. Large permanent collections have been set up in many countries including the USA, and exhibitions and conventions have become annual events for enthusiasts and the general public.

Today, "bonsai" has become a household word. There are hundreds of books in multiple languages about bonsai and related arts available worldwide. The small cuttings planted in shallow pots and sold in DIY stores and garden centers are very different from the bonsai that are produced by artists in Western countries, as well as Japan. They introduce newcomers to the idea of growing a miniaturized tree in a pot. It is then up to the individual, if sufficiently interested, to read books, join clubs, and meet and talk with other bonsai enthusiasts in order to learn how to maintain their bonsai.

BONSHO
BY RYUSHU SHUTAKU

A single tree growing on a single tray
The verdant green of one thousand years
Casting a dark, heavy shadow
Does anyone know
The vastness of that heaven and earth made from soil
The god of fire peak is within that tiny space.

OBTAINING BONSAI

The simplest way to start your collection is to buy a ready-made bonsai, one that has been imported from Japan, China, or Korea. This will give you that good feeling of having a tree to look at and care for. Do not spend too much money on your first tree; you have a lot to learn before you can be sure of keeping it healthy and in shape. If you can afford it, buy more expensive trees later, when you are more experienced.

Go to a specialist bonsai nursery (see Further Resources, page 140), not a garden center that has just a few unselected bonsai for sale in a small corner. They know and understand what they are selling, and can offer you expert advice and accurate care information. They want you to come back and buy more, so they will not sell you sick trees. A good specialist nursery will be very careful to stock only those species best suited as bonsai and that will thrive outdoors in our temperate climate. They will also likely sell a selection of tools, books, and magazines to help you care for your bonsai.

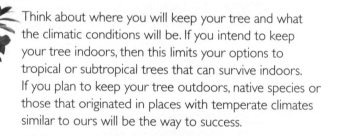

Think about where you will keep your tree and what the climatic conditions will be. If you intend to keep your tree indoors, then this limits your options to tropical or subtropical trees that can survive indoors. If you plan to keep your tree outdoors, native species or those that originated in places with temperate climates similar to ours will be the way to success.

Remember: small bonsai do not become big bonsai. You are in control; you grow them until they reach the desired size and trunk thickness and then trim and train them to retain that size. The ultimate challenge for the bonsai creator is to keep the essence of the tree.

Cherry blossom time (April) at a Japanese bonsai nursery.

WHAT TO LOOK FOR

The following are some of they key things to look for when selecting a ready-made bonsai tree.

An interesting-shaped trunk, not too straight, that tapers from the base to the apex. If buying a group planting, or "forest," the trunks should vary in height, width, and spacing.

An interesting arrangement of branches. The bottom third of the trunk should ideally be clear of branches.

Roots that are evenly distributed around the trunk and flare naturally as they enter the soil.

Existing pruning wounds should have been incorporated into the design of the tree, either by being carved into hollows, or by shaping and bleaching stubs of branches.

A tree with attractive colored or textured bark will always look better and reflect character.

Trees with naturally small and fine-textured leaves. It would take many, many years to get large leaves, like those of a chestnut, to reduce in size.

Evergreen trees, particularly pines and junipers, are a good choice because they stay green all year and naturally tend to have fine foliage.

RAW MATERIAL

If you get hooked on this absorbing hobby you will probably get more pleasure and certainly less expense from creating beautiful bonsai yourself. Go to your local garden center and choose something suitable—it will not cost a fortune. Buying a ready-made bonsai is like buying a dress from a shop. Buying a tree with the potential to be trained into a bonsai is like buying a roll of fabric, sewing pattern and a needle and thread. The age of the tree doesn't matter—it can be a seedling of one year or a 200-year-old tree dug from a cliff face.

WHAT TO AVOID

The following are some of the pitfalls to avoid when selecting ready-made bonsai or pre-bonsai material.

Prickly trees; you will regret it when you suffer later while training and trimming.

Small bonsai packaged for Christmas; they have been brought in from other climates (often subtropical), sealed in little, highly decorative boxes, and not opened for watering, and are unused to our climatic conditions.

Twisted, crossing, or uneven visible roots. These are very hard to rectify.

Poor graft unions. Some bonsai are grafted onto root stock of a similar variety. Scars from graft unions are permanent—if it is an ugly one, it is likely to get worse over time.

Packets of seeds or kits that state "Bonsai Seeds." There are no such things as "bonsai seeds," only tree seeds, the product of which can be trained to become bonsai. Unless you are very young, the chances of you producing a good bonsai from seed are as unlikely as growing Sherwood Forest from an acorn—it takes many, many years.

Yellowing or mottled foliage. This could indicate a number of health problems. Sick trees rarely, if ever, fully recover.

Evidence of pests and diseases. See pages 73–75 for some of the common problems that may affect bonsai.

A tree that isn't secure in its pot. This could indicate that the roots aren't filling the pot because they are not growing well, or have become waterlogged and are rotting. Test trees by gently trying to rock the trunk.

Old wounds that haven't been sealed properly. Decay may already have set in, which can be difficult to stop.

Wire scarring on branches. These weaken the tree and take many years to heal.

Many branches growing from the same point on the trunk; this could cause swelling of the trunk and be an ugly feature difficult to correct.

WHAT DO I NEED?

Your decision is made: you have fallen for these beautiful little trees and you want to try bonsai for yourself. You may even have taken advice and been out and bought one. Now you must not only keep it alive, but also learn how to progress with your tree, how to help it to become a fully developed, healthy work of art.

But what equipment are you going to need and what skills do you require to progress with this new hobby? You can manage, or make do, with tools you have at home, but if you want to take this seriously you need the right equipment. Remember the old saying "a bad workman always blames his tools." You don't want to have that as a valid excuse, so we need to get it correct from the start.

THE ESSENTIALS

Tools to work with in creating and shaping your trees.

Wire to assist in shaping the trees artistically.

Pots to contain your trees, and drainage screen to stop soil leaking out.

Soil or potting soil for the trees to grow in, and equipment such as sieves and scoops for mixing and placing soil.

Fertilizers to provide nutrients, and pesticides to keep your trees disease-free and healthy.

Wound paste, also known as tree paint or wound dressing. This can be applied after pruning or in places where the tree bark has been damaged. It helps to prevent bleeding (sap) and infection from airborne fungi.

Watering can and/or hose to provide moisture when nature doesn't.

Finally, lots of time and patience to give the bonsai the necessary care they deserve. Without this, do not take up the hobby—wait until you do have time. You would be unlikely to buy a puppy and then not allow time to take it on walks—the same applies to bonsai.

TOOLS

You can buy a whole set of top-of-the-range stainless steel bonsai tools; they almost look like works of art in themselves. But you do not need them—you can create equally good bonsai with just four or five basic steel tools. They may need cleaning and sharpening occasionally, but in other aspects they are the same. They are all standard tools for the purpose of work on bonsai, sold by any bonsai nursery or garden center as well as on the internet.

WIRE CUTTERS, for cutting wire. Ordinary domestic wire cutters do not get in close enough.

BRANCH CUTTERS, for cutting off branches that you do not require for your design. If you can afford it, it's also worth investing in concave branch cutters, which help to reduce scarring when cutting off branches close to the trunk.

SCISSORS, for small branch and twig trimming, as well as root trimming.

TWEEZERS, for weeding and removing dead foliage.

PLIERS, to hold wire and branches in place when wiring and shaping. Domestic pliers have a totally different gripping end, although you could "make do" using those to start with.

A TURNTABLE, for ease of rotating your bonsai while you are shaping it. This is useful, especially for a heavy bonsai, but not essential. A plastic turntable, 12in in diameter, is ideally suited for bonsai beginners.

WIRE

Wiring is crucial in training and styling bonsai trees. By wrapping wire around the branches of a tree, you can bend and reposition them.

It is important that you use the right material for wiring bonsai. Two types of wire are available: anodized aluminum and annealed copper, usually sold in 1-lb or 2-lb rolls and ranging in diameter from 0.8mm to 6mm.

For beginners, it is better to use the anodized aluminum; it is easier to work with and sold in most bonsai nurseries. It is available in different thicknesses, ranging from 1mm to 6mm diameter. You will probably only need 1mm, 1.5mm, 2.5mm, and 4mm-thick wire to start with. It is also about a quarter of the price of annealed copper wire, which only lasts a short time (annealing is a heat process that softens the wire; after a cold winter it will revert to hard and you will not be able to bend it effectively).

As a beginner you will use smaller quantities. You can only buy copper wire in 2-lb rolls, while aluminum wire can be bought in smaller quantities ranging from 1-lb right down to 4oz.

If you wire thick branches, it is a good idea to wrap them first with raffia; this will protect the branches from damage when bending them.

POTS

Bonsai literally means "a tree in a pot." The importance of selecting the right pot for your bonsai is underestimated—there are so many to choose from and getting the right one will transform your tree.

Many pots are imported from Japan, Korea, or China. Japanese pottery is known for its high quality and is often quite expensive, elegant, natural, and unglazed, whereas Chinese pottery is generally more ornate and cheaper, except for the rare and very costly antique pots. Today, a number of excellent European potters are competing well with the Japanese. If you have the money to splash out on an authentic Japanese or Chinese pot then by all means do so; but it is wiser to invest in the tree rather than the pot. You can buy bonsai pots in some garden centers, especially those that sell bonsai, but your choice will be limited. Specialist bonsai nurseries often supply pots, while bonsai potters will also have a selection or will make them specifically for you to suit individual trees.

SIZE MATTERS

Established bonsai trees, which have been root-pruned and repotted many times and no longer need regular training, have adapted to living in small pots. Younger trees, however, need more room to grow and will be trained step by step to adapt to living in increasingly smaller pots. This is done by pruning their roots every time they are repotted. They will therefore need slightly larger pots at first. Very new, immature trees can be planted in less expensive pots, widely available as training pots.

Choosing a pot that really suits the tree is difficult, as various factors have to be considered, such as shape, whether the pot is glazed or unglazed, and the color. A few basic guidelines (not rules, as choice is very personal), can be used to select the right pot:

WIDTH—Choose a pot with a width of about two-thirds the height of the tree.

DEPTH—The depth of the pot should be approximately equal to the thickness of the trunk base; young trees or those with very thin trunks are the exception to this (it would be hard to find a pencil-thin pot and also impractical to plant a bonsai in it).

SHAPE—For "masculine," heavy-looking strong trees, use angular pots. For more gently shaped "feminine," delicate-looking trees, use rounded pots.

GLAZE—Use unglazed pots for evergreen species, such as conifers and pine, and glazed pots for deciduous and flowering trees. Do not choose a bright glaze unless the tree has flowers or fruits.

DRAINAGE SCREEN

Placing drainage screen at the bottom of the pot prevents soil from being washed out through the drainage holes every time the bonsai is watered, which would result in the roots being exposed and the tree's health being put at risk. It also prevents slugs and other unwanted insects from sliding or crawling into the pot from beneath.

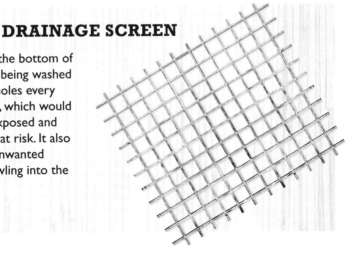

SOIL

A bonsai is confined to a relatively small quantity of soil, on which its very existence depends. The medium in which your bonsai is planted therefore plays a key role in whether it will thrive or die. If a bonsai looks unhealthy and lacks vigor, it is often because it has been planted in poor bonsai soil or, even worse, planted in normal garden soil, which hardens when it gets dry and cakes around the roots.

There are a number of requirements in a good soil mix:

GOOD WATER RETENTION—To be able to hold sufficient water to supply moisture between waterings.

GOOD DRAINAGE—Excess water must be able to drain from the pot. Lack of drainage can cause salts to build up and the roots to rot, killing the tree.

GOOD AERATION—The particles used in a bonsai mix should be large enough to allow plenty of tiny air pockets between each particle, which creates a network of pores that hold both air and water—essential for the development and sustenance of a healthy root system.

Mix approximately these quantities:
50% akadama
25% organic potting soil
25% grit

BONSAI SOIL MIXES

You can buy ready-mixed bonsai soils but they vary enormously from one supplier to the next; it is far safer and not a lot of trouble to mix your own. The most important components for any bonsai soil mixture are akadama, organic potting soil, and fine gravel (grit). Mix approximately these quantities: 50% akadama, 25% organic potting soil, and 25% grit.

AKADAMA is a baked Japanese clay, specifically produced for bonsai purposes. It often contains dust, which should be sifted out before use as it cakes once water is added. Akadama is usually sold in 30-lb bags and available in coarse, medium, and fine grades. Medium grade is the most commonly used. Cat litter, often referred to as "Kittydama," is a very good and much cheaper substitute and can be purchased in any supermarket—just be certain you do not buy one with an odor suppressant as it may contain chemicals that are harmful to your tree.

ORGANIC POTTING SOIL includes peat moss, perlite, and sand. It has disadvantages—used by itself, it retains water and doesn't aerate or drain very well—but as part of a mixture it works perfectly well.

FINE GRAVEL or grit is important to provide a well-drained, aerated bonsai soil. It can also be used as a bottom layer in pots to enhance drainage even further.

SIEVES AND SCOOPS

If you are going to mix your own soil, it's a good idea to buy a set of sieves and scoops for the purpose. You can, of course, make do with an old domestic sieve and spoons—as long as you don't then return them to the kitchen!

WATER

The most important part of taking care of your bonsai trees is watering. How frequently a tree needs to be watered depends on a number of factors, such as the species of tree, the size of tree, the size of pot, the time of year and the soil mixture. However, follow a few basic guidelines and you will soon learn to recognize when a tree needs to be watered.

WATER YOUR TREES WHEN THE SOIL GETS SLIGHTLY DRY

This means you should not water your tree when the soil is still wet but only when it feels slightly dry; use your fingers to check the soil about ½in down. In time you will be able to see (instead of feel) when a tree needs watering.

DO NOT WATER AS A ROUTINE

Check your trees regularly—do not simply water them on a daily routine, especially in damp weather.

USE THE RIGHT SOIL MIXTURE

The soil mixture greatly influences how often trees need to be watered. Trees in a good mixture of akadama, potting soil, and fine gravel should not become overwatered. However, if you buy trees in an unknown mix you need to watch them especially carefully.

There are myths that suggest you must not water when the sun is shining during the hottest part of the day or that you should never water with cold water. However, there are no real rules regarding the right time of day for watering. Trees are not that selective. The ground rule is: water as soon as the soil gets slightly dry!

Water with a fine rose-head watering can or hose, with not too much pressure, so as to guarantee fine, gentle watering that does not displace the soil. Water from above and keep watering until water runs out through the drainage holes.

THE PERILS OF OVERWATERING

The effects of under-watering are immediate and obvious. Overwatering is as bad but the effects take much longer to become noticeable and can often be difficult to diagnose. Overwatering creates an environment for the root system that is permanently wet. Roots need oxygen to "breathe" and the presence of too much water reduces the ability of the potting soil to absorb air. This in turn causes the fine root hairs to suffocate and die. The immediate effect to the tree is a loss of vigor as parts of its root system are unable to grow and they die back. The dead roots start to rot.

Naturally occurring bacteria are able to colonize the dead tissue and in very wet potting soils are able to thrive. Foliage on the tree will start to yellow and drop; smaller branches will shrivel and die back. As the live parts of the root ball become even smaller, it is eventually unable to support the primary branches and the trunk, causing the tree to die.

FOOD

Although bonsai are repeatedly pruned throughout their lives to retain their small stature, they should never be deprived of nutrients to stop them growing. Unable to reach down to subsoils, the tree will very quickly use up the nutritional content of the soil mixture; much nutrition is also lost during watering, when it is literally flushed out of the soil. A tree planted in the ground is able to extend its root system in search of nutrients, but a tree planted in a bonsai pot is dependent upon you to provide the necessary nutrients for its survival and good health.

WHAT PLANTS NEED

In order to grow, trees use carbon, hydrogen, and oxygen from the air and water from the soil to produce their own starch and sugars. They also need a number of simple chemicals from the soil, which they then use to create amino acids, proteins, vitamins, and enzymes.

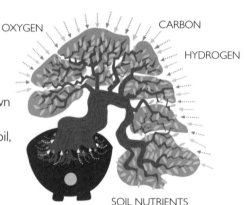

OXYGEN

CARBON

HYDROGEN

SOIL NUTRIENTS

SOIL NUTRIENTS

The three major plant nutrients required if plants are to grow satisfactorily are nitrogen, phosphorus, and potassium:

NITROGEN (N) is primarily used by plants for leaf growth.

PHOSPHORUS (P) in the form of phosphate (P2O5) is used by plants for root growth.

POTASSIUM (K) in the form of potash (K20) is used for flower and fruit production, and general hardiness.

In addition, there are various trace elements that all plants require, including iron (Fe), manganese (Mn), magnesium (Mg), Copper (Cu), cobalt (Co), and calcium (Ca).

FERTILIZERS

All good soils have a stock of nitrogen, phosphorus, and potassium; they come from the mineral part of the soil (sands, clays, and so on) and from dead organic matter (fallen leaves and dead plant matter). However, in the confines of a bonsai pot these vital elements are soon lost. The akadama and grit in bonsai soil mixes are usually completely lacking in these elements even before use. Therefore, regular use of fertilizer is required.

Manufactured fertilizers present a minefield of choice. Like human diet programs, there are no miracle pills. Basically, within the range they offer, they are very much alike and do an equally good job. Until you have a lot of experience and want to study the whole area in depth, you can simplify things for yourself by using the following "belt and braces" procedure:

1 Apply a good standard **slow-release fertilizer**. These are in the form of granules or pellets, coated with a porous material, which degrade slowly into the soil. Mix them into the soil or spread them on the surface and allow them to break down naturally. The warmer the soil, the faster this will take place; this corresponds to plant growth, which is faster in warm and damp weather. Apply the fertilizer at the beginning of the growing season and replenish it when needed (this varies according to the species—see Chapter 3: Species Profiles, pages 88–131). There is a range of slow-release products available, including "Osmocote" and "Miracle-Gro," and a number of Japanese products as well as organic chicken-manure pellets.

2 Use a good-quality **general liquid fertilizer**, which is well balanced with nutrients. Mix it with water and apply it to the whole of the soil surface (either with a watering can or a spray bottle—follow the packet instructions) until no more can be absorbed and surplus fertilizer runs out of the drainage holes of the pot. Do this every other week during the growing season.

APPLYING LIQUID FERTILIZER

Usage will vary according to the time of year and the needs of the tree. The ratio of each element varies according to the fertilizer. The principle ones are:

	Type of Feed	N2	P2O5	K
1.	High-Nitrogen	25	15	15
2.	Low-Nitrogen	2.5	25	25
3.	High-Potash	0	10	10
4.	Balanced	10	10	10

A HIGH-NITROGEN FEED is applied to many species during early spring, particularly when in training. The higher proportion of nitrogen encourages stronger root and leaf growth. It is not used during the growing season as this could result in too much lush green growth and long internodes.

A LOW-NITROGEN FEED is best applied in late summer through to dormancy. The relatively high potassium levels help to strengthen the year's growth and root systems before the cold of winter. It also helps with increased bud growth for the following year.

A HIGH-POTASH FEED (no nitrogen) is best applied in late fall when the tree has entered a state of dormancy. It has similar effects to that of a low-nitrogen feed.

THE BALANCED FEED with similar ratios of all three elements is a fertilizer applied during the growing season from late spring through to late summer.

AN ADDITIONAL FEED would be an agent with a 30: 10: 10 ratio, ideally suited for ericaceous or lime-hating plants, which prefer a slightly more acidic soil medium.

Pines and junipers particularly benefit from monthly "acid" feeds.

FOLIAR FEEDING

Foliar spraying is a valuable way to give your plants a balanced diet, by applying a number of different products to the leaves of the plant. The delicate leaf tissue will absorb the elements and put them to use immediately for an increased vigor in growth and fruit or flower development, plus an increased resistance to insects and fungal issues.

Care must be taken when applying foliar sprays. The concentration of elements must be more diluted in comparison to a root application. Results with foliar are almost immediate. If you are uncertain what elements are needed, use a foliar application of humic or fulvic acid. This will help the plant utilize the nutrients that you're already giving it through root feeding.

The most frequently used products are seaweed products (Nitrozyme, Maxicrop, Age Old Kelp). Seaweed contains a huge supply of natural hormones, and these hormones when applied to the leaves will cause increased growth rates and increased fruit or flower size.

HOW TO APPLY FOLIAR SPRAYS

• It is recommended to apply no more than twice a week.

• Aim for the leaves and stems of the plant, where the foliar feed is absorbed. They should not be dripping when you have finished applying; a light misting is all that is necessary to gain the benefits.

• Mist or lightly spray fruit or flowers to avoid drenching.

• For foliar feeding, there are often not instructions given on the product packaging. If this is the case, apply at a rate of 10 to 15 per cent of the maximum standard application instructions.

Avoid the really high N-P-K (see page 36) chemical nutrients, which are best left for root application.

Chapter 2

BONSAI
TECHNIQUES
AND CARE

It is time to get started with training, shaping, and styling your tree. This is the truly creative part of growing bonsai. It took many decades to refine techniques such as pruning and wiring to keep trees small, but the basics can be learned quickly and easily. In this chapter you will learn about the different styles of bonsai, how to care for your trees, when and how to style them, and what to do to keep them healthy.

BONSAI STYLES

Over the years, various naming systems having been proposed in order to classify bonsai trees. Most refer to tree shapes that can be observed in nature. The basic Japanese tree forms represented on the following pages have evolved as a way of categorising bonsai and also helping to establish basic guidelines for styling trees. Styles are usually grouped based on different criteria, such as the trunk orientation or the number of trunks in the bonsai specimen.

These styles are open to personal interpretation and creativity, meaning that trees do not necessarily need to conform to any specific category. However, to be able to classify them gives you the basis for understanding the shapes and should serve as guidelines for you to train your trees successfully.

BROOM
Hokidachi
The broom style is most suited for deciduous trees with extensive, fine branching. The trunk is straight and upright and does not continue to the top of the tree. The branches grow out in all directions from about one-third the height of the tree. The branches and leaves form a ball-shaped crown, which can look very dramatic during the winter months when the tree is without leaves.

BROOM

FORMAL UPRIGHT
Chokkan

This style occurs in nature when the tree stands alone and does not have to compete with other trees for light. This style has a completely straight, tapering, upright-growing trunk. The trunk must therefore be thicker at the bottom and grow increasingly thinner with the height. Branching should begin about a quarter to a third of the way up the length of the trunk. The top of the tree should be formed by a single branch. The branches leave the trunk alternately from left to right to back, with no branches pointing from the front until about the top third of the tree. All the branches will be fairly horizontal or slightly drooping, as if weighed down by snow in winter.

FORMAL UPRIGHT

INFORMAL UPRIGHT
Moyogi

The informal upright style is probably the most common both in nature and in the art of bonsai. The trunk grows upright roughly in the shape of a letter "S" and at every turn branching occurs. The branches should emerge on the outer curve of each bend and not the inside. Tapering of the trunk must be clearly visible, with the top or apex more or less directly above the base or the point at which the trunk emerges from the ground, and the base of the trunk thicker than the higher portion. The overall silhouette of an informal upright is often an irregular triangle.

INFORMAL UPRIGHT

DOUBLE TRUNK
Sokan

The double-trunk style is common in nature, but is not actually that common in the art of bonsai. Usually both trunks will grow out of one root system, but it is also possible that the smaller trunk grows out of the larger trunk just above the ground. The two trunks will vary in both thickness and length, the thicker and more developed trunk growing nearly upright, while the smaller trunk is a bit slanted. Both trunks contribute to a single crown of leaves, or canopy.

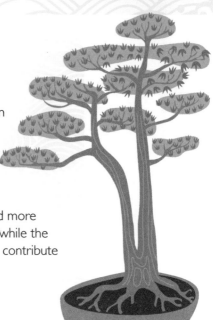

DOUBLE TRUNK

CLUMP

CLUMP, MULTI-TRUNK
Kabudachi

In theory, the multi-trunk style is the same as the double-trunk style, but with three or more trunks. All trunks grow out of a single root system, and it truly is one single tree. Trunks vary in width and height, but generally resemble each other in proportions, density of foliage, and other visual characteristics. One of the trunks (the thickest and most developed) will be dominant. The foliage atop each of the trunks joins to form one crown, with the foliage of the dominant trunk at the top.

RAFT

Netsumagari

This style copies a natural phenomenon that occurs when a tree topples onto its side. All the "new" trunks grow as branches from the previously upright trunk, and it truly is one single tree. The foliage atop each of the trunks joins to form one crown, with the foliage of the thickest, most developed trunk at the top. The original root system provides the branches with enough nutrients to survive. After a while, new roots will start growing from the underside of the original trunk, eventually taking over the function of the old root system.

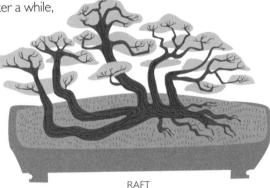

RAFT

FOREST

Yose-ue

The forest style looks a lot like the multi-trunk style, but the difference is that it comprises several individual trees rather than one tree with several trunks. The most developed trees are planted in the middle or slightly off center of a large, shallow pot. At the sides, a few smaller trees are planted to contribute to one single crown. The trees are planted not in a straight line but in a staggered pattern, because this way the forest will appear more realistic and natural.

FOREST

SLANTING

Shakan

This shape is usually the result of the wind blowing in one dominant direction or when a tree grows in shade and leans toward the light. The slanting-style trunk emerges from the soil at an angle, and the apex of the bonsai will be located to the left or right of the root base. The leaning angle should be about 60–80 degrees to the ground. The first branch grows opposite the direction of the tree, in order to create a sense of visual balance. The trunk can be slightly bent or completely straight, but should be thicker at the bottom than at the top.

SLANTING

WINDSWEPT

Fukinagashi

The windswept style is based on a shape that natural trees take when struggling to survive. The branches as well as the trunk grow to one side as if the wind has been blowing the tree constantly in one direction. The branches grow out all around the trunk but will all eventually be bent to one side.

WINDSWEPT

LITERATI

LITERATI

Bunjingi

In nature, this style of tree is found in areas with many other trees where competition for light is fierce, so that the tree can only survive by growing taller than all others around it. The trunk usually grows crookedly upward as it is heavy in relation to its height and is completely without branching because the sun only hits the top of the tree. In creating this style as bonsai, and to make sure that it looks tougher, some branches are "jinned," i.e. their bark is removed to achieve a deadwood effect (see pages 58–60). When the bark is removed from one side of the trunk, the exposed part of the trunk, which appears dead, is referred to as a "shari." The idea is to make it appear that the tree has had to struggle to survive. For aesthetic, these trees are often placed in small, round pots.

SHARI OR DRIFTWOOOD

Sharimiki

With the passage of time and harsh weather, such as lightning, winds, and storms, some trees lose the bark from sections of their trunks and branches die, shedding their foliage. The bark-less section (the "shari") usually begins at a point where the roots emerge from the ground, and grows increasingly thinner as it continues up the trunk. Intense sunlight will bleach these parts, forming a very characteristic feature of the tree. With bonsai, the bark is removed with a sharp knife and the bare area treated with lime sulfur in order to speed up the bleaching process (see pages 58–60). At least one strip of live bark must connect the leaves and living branches to the root system to transport water and nutrients.

SHARI OR DRIFTWOOD

CASCADE

CASCADE
Kengai

Modeled upon trees living in nature on a steep cliff or over water, where the trunk bends downward as a result of natural factors, like snow or falling rocks. It is not easy with bonsai to maintain a downward-growing tree because nature is directing it to grow upward. Cascade bonsai should be planted in raised pots. The tree should grow upright for a small distance but then bend downward. The crown or apex of the tree should grow approximately above the rim of the pot, with the subsequent branches alternating left and right on the outermost curves of an S-shaped trunk. These branches should be allowed to grow horizontally in order to maintain balance of the tree.

SEMI-CASCADE
Han-kengai

The semi-cascade style, like that of the cascade, is found in nature on cliffs and on the banks of rivers and lakes. The trunk grows upright for a small distance and then bends sideways and slightly down. Unlike the full cascade style, the semi-cascade trunk will never grow below the bottom of the pot. The apex is usually positioned above the rim of the pot while subsequent branching occurs below the rim.

SEMI-CASCADE

ROOT OVER ROCK
Seki-joju

On rocky terrain, trees are forced to search for nutrient-rich soil with their roots, which can often be found extending into crevices and holes in the rocks. Those roots exposed on the rock are unprotected before they reach soil level so they will develop a bark covering. With bonsai, the roots grow over a rock into the pot; ultimately the roots clasp onto the rock. Caring for this tree is little different from caring for any other style.

ROOT OVER ROCK

CREATING THE BASIC SHAPE

The aim of the initial pruning (sometimes called the "style-pruning") is to create the basic shape of your bonsai tree. (If you have bought a ready-styled tree, this part will have been done for you.) Do not repot your tree (see pages 70–72) until it has fully recovered.

AN EXAMPLE OF INITIAL STYLING

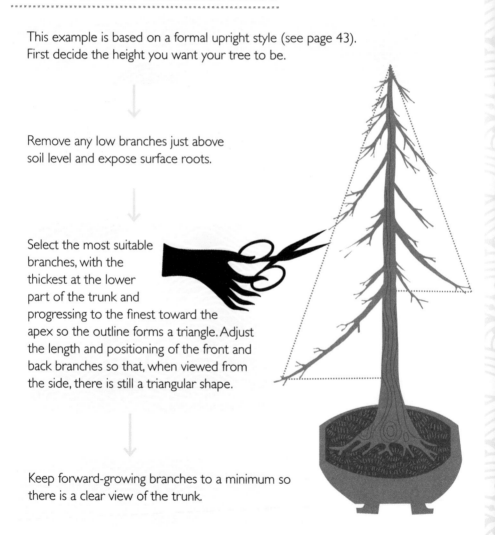

This example is based on a formal upright style (see page 43). First decide the height you want your tree to be.

Remove any low branches just above soil level and expose surface roots.

Select the most suitable branches, with the thickest at the lower part of the trunk and progressing to the finest toward the apex so the outline forms a triangle. Adjust the length and positioning of the front and back branches so that, when viewed from the side, there is still a triangular shape.

Keep forward-growing branches to a minimum so there is a clear view of the trunk.

BASIC SHAPES

The four illustrations below show four different examples of bonsai styles (see pages 42–49 for a list of the principle bonsai styles). In each instance, the use of a triangle surrounding the foliage can assist in creating a form appropriate to each of the styles, which in turn highlights a sense of balance and symmetry between the trunks and branches. The basic use of a triangle should be viewed as a guide to the shape being created rather than defining a precise silhouette of the bonsai.

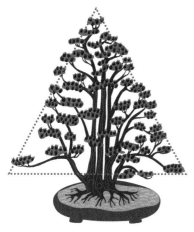

CLUMP, MULTI-TRUNK

FORMAL UPRIGHT

SLANTING

LITERATI

SHAPING BRANCHES

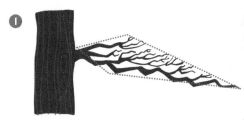

Each branch can be shaped as a diamond or triangle (Figures 1 and 2).

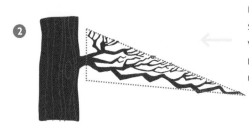

Where possible, wire and shape the main branch together with its secondary, smaller branches in such a way that, when viewed straight on, the main branch is visible on the underside of the branch arrangement.

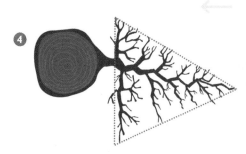

Figures 3 and 4 illustrate the diamond and triangular shape of the branch arrangements as viewed from above. The choice of shapes may well be determined by the number of secondary branches and their closeness to the trunk of the tree. In some instances, the species of tree and the style you choose may also determine choice.

PRUNING

Pruning is crucial for keeping trees miniaturized as well as for shaping them. The aim is to create a bonsai that resembles nature as closely as possible. Bonsai, being living, growing plants, need to be pruned from time to time to maintain their shape and, more importantly, their health and vitality. Pruning bonsai shoots lets in light and air, which helps strengthen and fortify the remaining leaves and branches and also encourages new growth; this in turn adds new and fresh sources of nourishment for the tree.

WHEN TO PRUNE

After the initial style-pruning, subsequent pruning is to maintain and refine the shape of the tree you have created. Trees will concentrate most growth on the top and outer parts. It is important to prune these areas regularly in order to encourage growth closer to the inner parts of the tree; a healthy tree will have no problem coping with pruning up to a third of its branches. Most experts agree that you only do this once a year. Preferably, just before the growth season is the right time to style-prune a tree. You can check your particular tree in Chapter 3: Species Profiles (pages 88–131), as some do vary slightly.

BUXUS SEMPERVIRENS (BOX)

GETTING THE RIGHT BALANCE

When pruning, remember that a balance must be struck. A bonsai must be allowed to grow. New growth is not only a sign of a healthy bonsai but, in turn, it generates a fresh view of the tree's structure, new root growth, and vitality. Therefore a bonsai must be allowed periods of growth—enough to revitalize its energy but not so much that growth becomes coarse or the shape of the tree is completely lost and apical dominance is allowed ("apical" means top or uppermost part of the tree).

HOW TO PRUNE

Make sure you have the right tools (see pages 28–29). Place the tree on a table at eye level. Use your turntable if you have one; this is of more value for larger trees that are difficult to lift and turn by hand. The first stage is to remove all the dead material from the tree. Take your time; observe your tree and decide which branches do not fit the desired design (see pages 56–57 for a guide).

You want to cut the branches, not break them, as this would leave severe unsightly scars. The angle of cut is not an issue unless you wish to remove a branch completely—in this case, cut it flush with the trunk or, preferably, use a special concave branch cutter to avoid creating an ugly scar. Pruning thick branches will also result in ugly scars, but by using a concave cutter you will reduce this effect significantly; the indentation it makes when cutting off the branch hollows out the trunk slightly and allows it to heal over with a flatter scar.

If reducing the length of a branch, do not cut too close to a potential bud as there could be dieback and the bud would be lost (this is common with acers).

Finally, it is advisable to seal large cuts with wound paste. The paste, containing a fungicide, protects the wounds against infections and helps the tree to heal faster.

WHAT TO PRUNE

It is not possible to tell you which branches to prune without actually seeing the tree. A few simple guidelines are listed below, but deciding on the future design of your tree is a creative process for you; do not be bound by rules.

- If two branches occur at the same level on the tree, keep one and remove the other.
- Remove branches with unnatural twists and turns.
- Remove disproportionately thick branches from near the top of the tree.
- Remove any branches growing vertically from an existing branch; trees naturally grow toward light, but this does not lead to an artistic form.
- Remove branches that conceal the front view of the trunk.

UNDESIRABLE BRANCHES

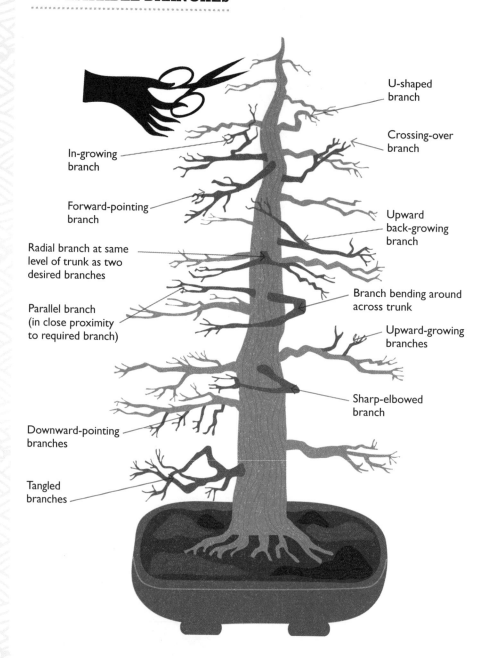

U-shaped branch

Crossing-over branch

In-growing branch

Forward-pointing branch

Upward back-growing branch

Radial branch at same level of trunk as two desired branches

Branch bending around across trunk

Parallel branch (in close proximity to required branch)

Upward-growing branches

Sharp-elbowed branch

Downward-pointing branches

Tangled branches

TREE AFTER PRUNING

DEADWOOD ON BONSAI

Creating deadwood on bonsai, in the form of jin (dead branch) or shari (hollowed trunk), can significantly improve the appearance and character of the tree. These add an effective feature to the design of many old pines and junipers.

Jins on trees in nature are normally created when branches are broken by winds, by the weight of snow or by lightning strikes. It is a natural feature on coniferous trees that the lower branches die back; shaded from the light, these branches rot away—all that remains are short stubs of deadwood.

GETTING STARTED

The process of creating a jin is straightforward, but getting the design right can be more difficult. A successful jin should appear as though it has been created by nature. Use branches that are not required as part of the foliage mass, and do not create too many on one tree, as it will look unnatural. Jins only work on coniferous trees; deciduous wood is usually softer and would rot away rather than "jin."

First of all, ensure you have the correct tools— "making do" is not an option, you will only cause disfiguring damage. You will require: a small, very sharp, pointed knife; bonsai pliers (ordinary pliers are not the correct design); hand wood-engraving chisels (only use electric ones when you have had experience); and lime sulfur for whitening the wood. All these items are available from bonsai stores.

Practice first on unwanted old branches, not on trees you wish to keep.

CREATING A JIN

Select the branch you want to jin. Using a sharp knife, slice through the bark close to the trunk. Using jinning pliers, crush the bark on the branch so it can be peeled off easily.

Using a branch splitter or branch cutter, begin to cut away parts of the branch to create the impression of a dead branch that has broken off.

With the jinning pliers, pull away slivers of the wood; this reveals the grain of the wood, giving a natural appearance to the jin. If necessary, smooth off the exposed wood of the jin with sandpaper.

Bleach the jin with lime sulfur and leave to dry. Do this step outside as the smell is lingering and noxious. When first applied, the lime sulfur gives a deep yellow color; on drying out, it becomes a gray-white color, giving the impression of dead wood exposed over many years.

CREATING A SHARI

The full correct term is *sharamiki*, meaning deadwood. Do not overdo this; it is a job for the experienced and those knowledgeable enough horticulturally not to "ringbark" accidentally and consequently kill the tree. Experiment with very small areas of stripped and hollowed trunk; if you are successful, you can try more later.

Choose the right spot on the trunk for a shari—one that not only looks good but also does not cut off supplies of nutrients to branches higher up the tree. Before you start removing bark, draw the desired shape of the shari on the trunk with chalk or a pen.

Start by taking just a narrow strip of bark; you can widen it in stages. Be careful not to remove a complete strip around the circumference of the trunk (ring barking) as this would sever the xylem and phloem and result in the death of the tree. A shari should be (ideally) only down one side of the trunk. Outline the shape and cut through the bark with a sharp knife, tearing the bark down using jin pliers.

Hollow out the defined shape with carving tools to the depth you initially feel safe doing; you can deepen it later.

Bleach the area with lime sulfur—this acts to protect against infection as well.

WIRING

Wiring is an absolutely crucial technique to train and style bonsai trees. By wrapping aluminum or copper wire around the branches of a tree, you are able to bend and reposition the trunk and branches into your desired shape.

You will need flexible, non-rusting wire (see page 29) of several different gauges; the thickest you are likely to use is 4mm. For smaller branches and young trees you will only require 1–2mm.

WHEN TO WIRE

Wiring can be done year-round for most tree species. During the growth season, branches thicken quite quickly and as a result the wire will cut into the bark, creating ugly scars. Check on your tree regularly and remove the wire in good time to prevent scarring. It will take a few months before the branches are set in their new shape. The wire should then be cut off, not unwound, as this may well damage the branches.

GUY WIRES

Occasionally, when wiring the branches of a bonsai, thicker branches can require a considerable amount of wire to bend them as required. This can be both damaging to the branch as well as unsightly. To avoid excessive wiring when working on a thicker branch, attach a fine wire to the end of the branch and pull it down to the appropriate position. The other end of the wire can then be attached to either a lower branch or, preferably, a heavy exposed root at the level of the soil surface. Ensure that the wire around the branch has a small rubber pad to prevent it cutting in to the branch over time.

WIRING THE TRUNK

Cut a length of wire, probably about 3mm diameter (unless the trunk is very thick) and about 25 per cent longer than the actual trunk length. Insert one end deeply into the soil near to the trunk, carefully avoiding damage to the roots, and use this as the anchoring point.

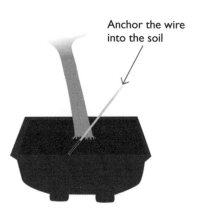

Anchor the wire into the soil

Coil the wire gently and not too tightly around the tree between the branches at an angle of approximately 45 degrees until you reach the top of the trunk.

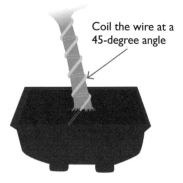

Coil the wire at a 45-degree angle

Very gently bend the trunk to the desired shape, stopping immediately if the wood shows signs of splitting. You can always bend it further the next year when the wood has recovered.

WIRING A BRANCH

Wire each branch in the same way as you wired the trunk, choosing a grade of wire to suit the thickness of the branch. Attach the wire to the trunk or to the opposing branch but be careful not to cross any wire on the trunk as this may bite into the bark, causing scarring. The wire should be thick enough to hold the branch in its new shape. Wire all the branches you intend to shape before actually starting to bend and position them.

Similarly, when more than one length of wire is necessary in wiring the trunk or carrying wire from the trunk to a branch, ensure that the wires run parallel to each other. Do not allow wires to cross. This could have an adverse effect later, especially if one of those wires has to be removed and the other retained.

Very gently bend the branches to their desired position. A gentle downward slope of the branch creates an impression of age. Hold the outside of the branch with your fingers, then bend the branch from the inside of the curve with your thumbs. This way you reduce the risk of splitting branches. When a branch is in position, stop moving it as repeated bending will probably damage the branch. Try to bend straight sections of branches slightly to make the whole thing look more natural.

SECONDARY AND TERTIARY WIRING

When wiring a branch that has smaller secondary and even finer tertiary branches, different gauges of wire should be used. Start with the thickest wire, attached to the trunk and going part of the way along the branch, before changing to a finer wire on the smaller secondary branches, and, if necessary, even finer wire toward the tips of each of the finest branches. As far as possible, run the different wires in parallel to avoid any wire crossing.

ORIGINAL
BRANCH

WIRING THE
PRIMARY BRANCH

WIRING THE
SECONDARY BRANCHES

WIRING THE
TERTIARY BRANCHES

WIRING IN PAIRS

A useful technique is to wire two branches with the same piece of wire; this avoids both loose ends of wire that must be attached and the inevitable crossed wires.

First select the pair of branches you need to wire; these have to be of similar thickness and near each other on the tree. The wire should wrap around the trunk at least once (preferably twice) so the wire will not move when bending the branches later on.

Cut off the right length of wire to wrap around both the branches.

Continue wiring to the tip of the first branch

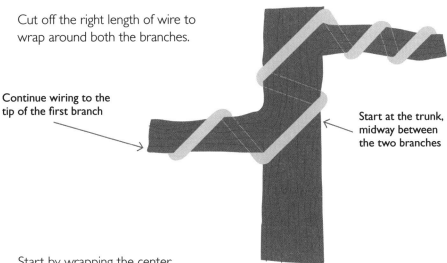

Start at the trunk, midway between the two branches

Start by wrapping the center point of the wire around the trunk and proceed to the first branch. Wire from the trunk end of the branch to the very tip before starting to wire the other branch. The wire should be wrapped around the branches at an angle of 45 degrees.

If you intend to bend the branch downward, make sure the wire comes from below. If you intend to bend the branch upward, the wire should come from above.

WIRING THE WHOLE TREE

When wiring an entire tree, work from the trunk to the primary branches and then start wiring the secondary branches.

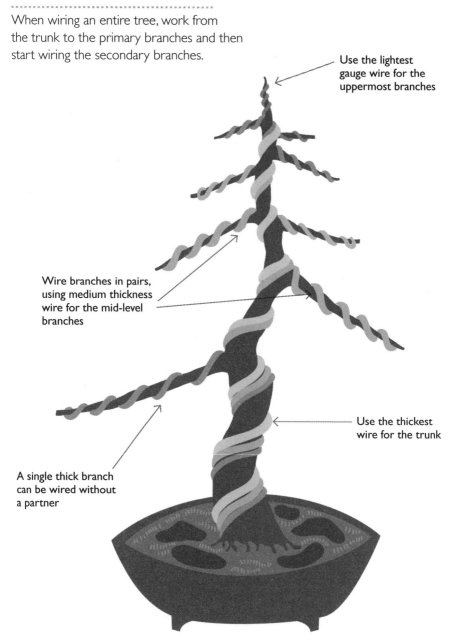

Use the lightest gauge wire for the uppermost branches

Wire branches in pairs, using medium thickness wire for the mid-level branches

A single thick branch can be wired without a partner

Use the thickest wire for the trunk

REPOTTING:
WHY AND WHEN TO DO IT

Repotting is probably the most important exercise involved in the successful cultivation of bonsai trees. Unfortunately, it is also the least studied and understood, and therefore poorly done; it is not just a simple matter of placing a tree in a new mix in a different pot. Repotting is done for the long-term health and well-being of the tree. With bonsai, the more root the tree has, the faster the tree can grow and the better it will develop.

WHY REPOT?

Unlike animals, plants do not eat food; they seem to create it from virtually nothing. In order to live, plants need water, carbon dioxide, and sunlight. These are required for photosynthesis, the means by which plants create carbohydrates (starch and sugars) in their leaves. Carbohydrates are burned in a process called respiration; this drives cell division and the plant grows. Respiration needs oxygen and the process creates carbon dioxide and water as by-products. If insufficient oxygen is available, the process produces alcohol, which is toxic to the tree. Oxygen is readily available above ground but it is harder to acquire within the soil around the roots. This is the reason that repotting is so necessary and why, without it, the tree can die.

SIGNS THAT A BONSAI IS READY FOR REPOTTING

There are no absolute rules for this; it must involve a good share of common sense. More often than not, the trigger for repotting will be when you want the tree to grow larger and you need a bigger pot or when you find a pot more to your liking or more suitable. With these exceptions, the general rule for repotting is every one to five years, depending on the species of tree and the size of the container or pot. Fast-growing trees need to be repotted every year or every other year. More mature trees need to be repotted every three to five years. Any of the following are a sign that the tree needs repotting:

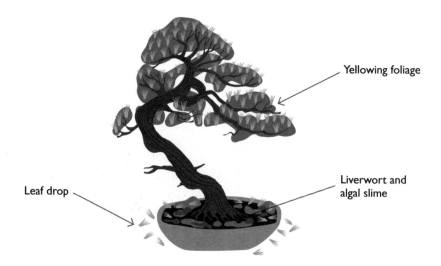

Yellowing foliage

Liverwort and algal slime

Leaf drop

- The roots are pushing the tree upward out of the pot.

- Water is not absorbed by the soil and just runs off the surface. This means the soil has compacted and the tree is pot-bound.

- A slowing of growth compared with last year.

- Reduced uptake of water in summer.

- Rapidly reducing leaf size.

- Leaf drop in summer and early leaf drop in fall.

- Yellowing of foliage.

- Fine twigs dying back in winter.

- Liverwort and algal slime forming on the soil surface.

CHECKING THE ROOTS

Do not repot on a routine basis—instead, check on your trees in late winter or early spring by carefully removing the tree from its pot. A bonsai needs to be repotted when the roots circle around the root system against the inside of the pot. If the roots still have room to grow within the soil, wait another year before checking again.

WHEN TO REPOT

Repotting should be done during the early spring, when the tree is still in dormancy. This way, the somewhat damaging effect of repotting is reduced to a minimum, as the tree does not yet have to sustain a full head of foliage. Repotting in early spring will also ensure that damage done to the root system will be repaired as soon as the tree starts growing.

ROOT PRUNING

The roots of a bonsai will develop and eventually fill the pot in which it stands. When this happens, the tree is said to have become "pot-bound." This necessitates having to take the tree out of its pot in order to trim back excess roots, especially those growing in a circle around the inside of the pot. Root pruning is also appropriate if the tree's roots are tight to the edge of the pot. In this instance, cut back the roots so that when you place the tree back in its pot there is sufficient space to put fresh soil around the inside edge. This will then allow the tree to develop new, finer fibrous roots and permit the tree to grow more strongly.

HOW TO REPOT YOUR BONSAI

Before starting the repotting process, allow the tree to dry out a little; working with wet soil is very difficult.

Choose the new pot (see page 31). It will usually be larger than the old pot, unless you are going from a flowerpot to your first bonsai pot. Again, the amount of root will determine pot size when going from smaller to larger. How much larger? Choose what looks right for the tree—aim to create a harmonious balance between tree and pot.

Prepare the new pot. Place the screen under the drainage hole. Wrap the center point of a long length of wire around a wooden dowel, repeat with a second length, and feed the four ends through the drainage screen and into the pot. Pull so that the dowel is tight against the underside of the pot beneath the drainage hole. Be sure the wire is long enough for the ends to be exposed above the edge of the pot to secure the tree in place.

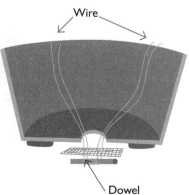

Wire

Dowel

Begin filling the base of the pot with coarse grit, distributed evenly.

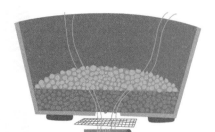

Take the tree out of its old pot, using a sharp knife to cut around the edge if it is stuck.

Using a root hook or sharp pointed object, carefully remove the soil and disentangle the roots. When repotting pine trees, never remove all the soil; this would remove the mycorrhizal fungus, which is essential for the tree's survival.

Cut back long roots; this will help your tree to grow a more compact, fibrous root system. Also remove any rotting or vertical-growing roots. Prune up to a quarter of the total root mass.

Place the tree in the pot, with two lengths of wire on either side of the roots. Think about the style of the tree when choosing its position in the pot. Unless the tree itself is symmetrical in shape, such as a broom-style bonsai, it is usually best to place it slightly off center.

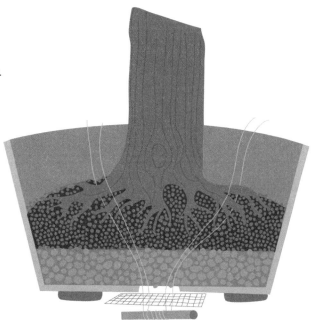

Secure the tree in position with the wires, twisting the ends together to anchor the tree.

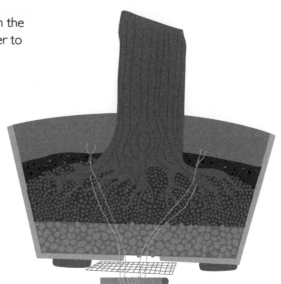

Fill the pot using a soil mixture (see pages 32–33) to about ½in below the rim. Make sure the soil is compact and no air pockets are left between the roots.

Water the tree thoroughly—this will settle the soil and fill up any remaining air pockets.

After repotting, keep the tree protected from frost and do no other work on it until it has had an opportunity to recover. This will vary for different trees, but wait until the tree shows evidence of new growth.

PESTS AND DISEASES

Most plant problems cause symptoms that are easy to spot. A bonsai may wilt, become discolored, or fail to bloom or even fail to come into leaf at all. What causes this to happen? It could be because the tree hasn't been watered sufficiently or maybe a delicate tree has been exposed to harsh weather. If neither of these, it is most likely to be some form of pest or disease.

PESTS: Creatures that cause damage to cultivated plants, the largest group of which are the insects. They feed in different ways—by sap-sucking, leaf-mining, defoliating, or tunneling through stems. Some pests damage plants by spreading viral or fungal diseases. Others coat plants with a sugary excrement that encourages the growth of sooty molds.

DISEASES: Diseases are caused by pathogens and spread by a carrier—the most common carriers are air currents or water. Very few pathogens are commonly carried by insects, such as aphids.

APHIDS

Aphids are sap-sucking bugs. It is usually easy to see aphid infestations with the naked eye; they colonize shoot tips, flower buds, and the underside of younger leaves. Aphids can cause stunted growth with curled or distorted leaves. This can weaken the plant. Many aphids also excrete a sticky honeydew, which allows the growth of black sooty molds. When an infestation is spotted, insecticides should be used regularly and thoroughly.

VINE WEEVILS

Adult weevils resemble little dark gray beetles about ½in long with a long snout. An adult weevil needs two to three weeks of feeding before it begins to lay eggs. It then alternately feeds and lays eggs for about a month. Weevils are most active at night—during the day, the adult hides in dark places on the stems of very dense plants. Apart from nibbling circular indentations into the leaves, the adults cause little more than aesthetic damage. Simply pick them off by hand as and when they are seen. It is the larvae (or grubs) that cause the worst harm. They feed on the roots and exist purely

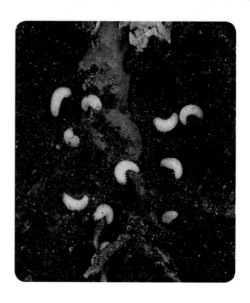

in the soil, so you probably won't even know they are there until the tree starts to die. Larval feeding starts in spring and continues into fall. The larvae can be controlled by a chemical drench that is watered on: follow the manufacturer's instructions for safe and effective application. Note that vine weevil adults do not necessarily feed on the same plant where they lay their eggs.

RED SPIDER MITES

These mites are microscopic in size and extremely harmful. Ultimately the damage from these creatures may cause the tree to die if not treated. Found on the lower surface of leaves, they breed best in warm, dry conditions. Look for silk webbing and discoloration of leaves, and then leaf drop. Difficult to control, red mites breed rapidly and some strains are resistant to some pesticides. Use insecticidal soap spray at three- to five-day intervals until new growth appears unaffected. Even if treatment with a pesticide has been successful, affected leaves will remain mottled and the cast skins of the mites may still be visible.

WOOLLY APHIDS

A small, white, fluffy insect about $\frac{1}{16}$in long, which feeds by sucking the sap of many species. Because of its conspicuous appearance, the woolly aphid is easy to spot. The aphids disappear over winter, leaving behind tiny eggs, which hatch in the spring. The newly hatched aphids then become active again, sucking sap from beneath the bark, and start secreting their fluffy "wool." They make plants sticky and messy. Scrub the aphid colonies with a stiff-bristled brush or spray regularly with a systemic insecticide throughout the growing season, and again in late winter.

FUNGAL INFESTATIONS

This covers a whole group that individually are quite hard to identify. They are similar in the symptoms they cause, and they make the plant unsightly with damaged foliage and impaired growth, and are sometimes even seriously harmful to the trees. These infestations include rust, powdery mildew, and the browning and dropping of needles, all associated with warm, damp conditions. If a foliar fungal disease such as powdery mildew or rust is identified then it may be appropriate to apply a systemic fungicide. Ensure that fungicides are applied correctly by following the instructions on the label. Burn or bin the dead foliage (far away from your trees) as the microscopic fungal spores will live on to re-infest unless you dispose of them effectively.

SEASONAL MAINTENANCE

Bonsai are the same as any other growing plant—they respond to the seasons. Thus you need to respond to nature: during the warm months, when your bonsai are growing, trim or prune them; during cold and frosty conditions, protect them.

SPRING MONTHS

As soon as spring starts you can remove your trees from their winter quarters and place them outside. Harden them off and move them from their winter quarters.

MARCH

Repotting deciduous trees can be done now, but be sure the early starters, such as the elm and some maples, have not yet shown signs of opening buds.

Most trees can be left unprotected now, unless freezing winter temperatures are still continuing; any insulating materials used can be removed in late March. Most pine trees can still be repotted until late March.

APRIL

Most trees are now growing; a few species are slower starters and take more time, such as the oak. As the trees are growing strongly, a feeding regime can be resumed. Trees can now be repotted, trained, and pruned.

For most trees, this is the best time to start wiring, but watch if trees grow rapidly; check on your wiring so it doesn't cut into the bark.

MAY

Growing trees can now be trained.

Feeding is very important now. Water daily, unless the weather is very wet. Infestations of aphids are frequent, especially if it is a moist, damp spring, so be ready with your bug gun.

Watch your azaleas: they will be flowering soon. Do not cut off growth or you may destroy this year's flowers.

Treat all your trees with vine weevil drench. This is the time that larvae emerge to begin their life cycle.

SUMMER MONTHS

Summer is the main and most important growing season.

JUNE

A busy time; your trees are truly growing now. Regular pruning of new growth is necessary. New growth will mean the trunk and branches are growing thicker. Watch wire carefully to be sure it does not cut in and scar the bark.

Weeds grow very strongly as well—do not let them get the upper hand or they will take all the nutrients from the soil.

Days are long and nights short—perfect growing conditions. Sometimes you may need to water twice in a day.

Barbecue time—do not set up barbecue grills near your trees; the trees can scorch easily.

JULY

This should be the warmest month of the year (not always, though!). Check for watering regularly.

Pinch and prune fine twigs: this involves the removal of shoots, leaves, and stems to direct and control growth, increase branch density, and encourage the formation of foliage "pads." This helps to make leaves smaller and reduce internodes.

Keep feeding—it may be a good time to try foliar feeding, a fine mist feed taken in by the foliage (see page 39).

Be prepared for sudden thunderstorms; hail and strong winds can be very damaging, especially to new leaves and flowers.

AUGUST

Check your trees for bugs and insects.

If you are going on holiday, do not just abandon your trees—they could be dead when you come home. Ask a reliable neighbor to water your bonsai for you.

ADDITIONAL SUMMER TIPS

Your bonsai tree's chances of survival depends on watering. A day or two of neglect and the root ends will die. There is an old Japanese saying: "water your bonsai tree three times—once for the pot, once for the soil, and once for the tree," so go back and forth three times. This allows the water to soak into the soil and the pot, leaving sufficient water for the tree to take in.

- Avoid the temptation to water your bonsai trees just to "cool them down" as it ultimately does more damage than good. Each drop of water will act like a little magnifying glass, focussing the sun's rays onto the foliage.

- The increased amount of watering during the summer means that nutrients stay around for a relatively short time, as they will be washed out through the well-drained soil. Keep feeding regularly and often.

- Position your trees to receive a good amount of sun but also some afternoon shade. The pot itself can rise to temperatures in the afternoon sun that will cook the tree's roots.

- Don't let your plants get out of control, especially the faster growers such as junipers and elms. Keep new growth pinched back before it gets too long, so that you don't lose the shape you've spent time working on. Trim any tight growth to allow sufficient air circulation and light.

- If a bonsai gets wilted leaves, put it in the shade and give it a little water. Give the tree a little more water later that day. Let the roots recover slowly—don't drown them.

- Too much sun and too little water will result in leaf curl and browning. If a bonsai is not taken care of daily during summer the leaves will die and fall off, and then the plant could die. With the heat of the summer, your bonsai tree will stop producing new leaves. Do not lose the ones that are there.

FALL MONTHS

During the fall, trees start preparing for the coming winter by hardening up new growth and, for deciduous trees, by dropping leaves to reduce moisture loss.

SEPTEMBER

Fertilize outdoor trees for the last time with a low-nitrogen feed, to harden off their growth and prepare them for the coming winter. Give all your trees another drenching with proprietary vine weevil drench. Any surviving larvae could eat a lot of the fine roots over winter and cause catastrophic damage.

OCTOBER

Fall colors on outdoor trees are at their best now.

Protect your more delicate trees from cold nights.

At the end of the month, start to clean up for winter. Remove all dead leaves, weed, and remove excess moss from the surface—it could make the trees over-wet in the winter. Use a good lime sulfur winter wash and spray your trees to remove algae and minimize the risk of bugs settling in corners of the pot for winter.

NOVEMBER

Bonsai, although hardy, do appreciate protection from the worst of the frost and drying winter winds from mid November to February. So now is the time to prepare your storage area or greenhouse. Clean, remove debris, and power-wash greenhouses and polytunnels. A protected spot in the garden, cold frame, cold greenhouse, or unheated porch can be used for winter storage; do not overprotect. Do not bring trees into the house, unless they are tropical. Bonsai need a dormant period to survive.

WINTER MONTHS

The trees are now going into dormancy, the period of least growth.

DECEMBER

Keep your trees well protected from freezing temperatures.

Keep checking the soil—your trees might require watering in the absence of rain.

Enjoy Christmas but do not forget your trees in all the excitement.

Look at your trees while they are not in leaf—you can then better see the structure and determine the future shape.

JANUARY

Probably one of the worst months of the year for your bonsai. During the winter, most trees need to be well protected from long periods of freezing temperatures. Place in a cold greenhouse or polytunnel or cover them with insulating material such as horticultural fleece. If there is little or no rain, occasional watering should keep them moist but not wet.

Shohin and mamé, or smaller size trees, should be under cover—this allows for better control of moisture levels.

FEBRUARY

Keep checking for insects, particularly on deciduous trees (such as the oak). To overcome these unwanted elements, give each bonsai a lime sulfur wash. You will have done this before the winter started and can now do it again. This helps eliminate the risk of infestation of pests and onset of disease.

Outdoor trees will consume little water but watering might be required in the absence of rain.

If watering is necessary, ensure that it is done early in the day; this allows time for drainage should temperatures drop below freezing at night.

ADDITIONAL WINTER TIPS

Most bonsai, although hardy, do appreciate protection from the worst of the winter weather. A protected spot in the garden, cold frame, cold greenhouse, or unheated porch can be used for winter storage. Only bring tropical trees into the house and then not into hot, centrally heated rooms, nor on window sills behind curtains where the temperatures can drop to almost outside temperatures.

- Do not overprotect your bonsai. During the winter, trees naturally go into a period of dormancy that is essential to their health the following year.

- Be careful not to let your trees get confused and think winter is over; this will result in them starting to come out of dormancy. Imagine the nasty shock when it gets cold again and the trees have started to bud: the buds will die off. Keep them protected until it really is spring.

- Be vigilant against top growth damage, which occurs when the temperature rises during the day while the water in the ground or pot is still frozen. This can often arise in greenhouses where there are large fluctuations in temperature between day and night. As temperatures rise, the leaves start to transpire but the roots are unable to take in replacement water from the frozen soil, causing the top growth to dry out and die back. It can also be aggravated by wind, which causes moisture loss from leaves and shoots.

- Ensure your bonsai are sheltered from the wind. Winter winds combined with temperatures below 23°F will freeze-dry almost any bonsai.

- Bear in mind that lower light levels can be acceptable during dormancy. Dormant deciduous trees have no leaves and do not need light until they start growing. Dormant evergreens do not need much light as long as the temperature does not rise above 41°F for very long. Evergreens stored in the dark at temperatures around or below freezing (32°C) will survive the winter.

GROUP PLANTINGS

Although bonsai are most commonly grown and displayed as solitary trees, in nature trees are more commonly seen in groups as forests or woodlands, so why not produce bonsai in this truly natural way? Group plantings can replicate a number of trees growing together in a copse, wood, or forest and reflect the interplay between the trees and their branches as they compete for light and nutrients. We all lead full, busy lives and how much time do we have to wander in the woods to listen to the birds and admire the beauties of nature? These miniature forests can fill us with wonder and tranquillity, all in a single tray in our own back yard—a very good reason to grow your own forest planting.

While it can take years of training to create a good image of a mature tree with an individual bonsai, a well-designed group can be produced really quite rapidly from young immature saplings. Successful groups can be created using young, thin-trunked plants that would otherwise take many years to become good individual bonsai specimens. Successful group plantings are not so reliant on the material used; it is the artist's creativity that makes for satisfying results.

Most species can be used for group plantings, though species that have naturally upright branching habits are preferable. Small-leaved varieties are probably most suited as reducing leaf size takes a long time. Particularly recommended are beech, birch, cryptomeria, elms, zelkova, hornbeam, juniper, larch, maples, olives, and ficus (fig).

CREATING A GROUP PLANTING

A bonsai group planting creates an illusion of perspective by using a number of visual tricks. Perspective is created by drawing the eye to a number of focal points that subconsciously fool the viewer. Be sure to choose healthy, well-rooted trees of the species you decide to use and ensure you have a range of heights and thicknesses of trunk; shape is not too important, as you can adapt it. The spring is the best time of year to create a group planting.

DESIGNING A GROUP PLANTING

Before you get to work assembling your group planting, it is a good idea to assess your trees carefully and sit down with pencil and paper to roughly plan the composition of the planting. Here are some tips to bear in mind:

Tall trees are positioned at the front of the pot and smaller trees toward the back, creating a feeling of greater perspective.

Trees in nature vary in height and trunk thickness and this should be reflected in your design; the tallest trees should have the thickest trunks, the smallest trees the thinnest. Try to avoid symmetry in group planting as this will look unnatural; trees should be planted at unequal distances from each other and according to height.

DRAWING THE EYE

A sense of perspective can also be created by creating subgroups of trees so that the entire group will consist of two, three, or more smaller groups. The viewer's eye is then drawn through the trunks of the planting to the smallest trees at the back, which reinforces the sense of perspective.

The eye is drawn to the smaller trees

Gap creates a sense of space

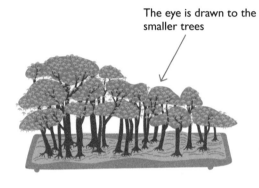
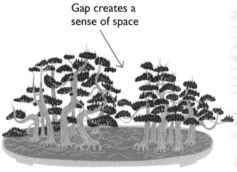

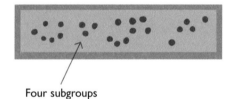

Four subgroups

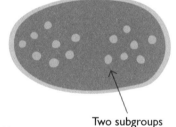

Two subgroups

The silhouette of the planting as a whole should be triangular, with the two sides from the apex, or top, tapering away at different angles. If the silhouette of the background trees is kept simple, attention is drawn to the trunks and branches of the trees at the front, the rear trees becoming less distinct and therefore seeming further away.

PREPARING THE POT OR TRAY

Initially, you can use inexpensive plastic trays. At a later stage you can buy a proper group planting pot or perhaps even have one custom made from fiberglass, concrete, resin, or wood. Make sure it is large enough so that the trees won't be crowded, allowing for space to divide it into sections—imagine paths through the woodland.

The container can be oval or rectangular or an irregular slab. The only serious rule is that it must be shallow and have good drainage holes. Cut them yourself with a drill if they are not there already.

Cover the drainage holes with screen and fix it in position with wire (see page 31).

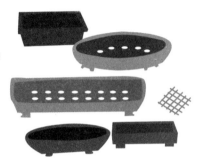

Cut several pieces of wire (about 4in long) and attach these to the pot using the drainage holes (see the wire and dowel technique on page 70). The wires will be used to anchor the roots and stabilize the composition of the trees.

Place a thin layer of small gravel across the whole container to ensure good drainage.

PREPARING THE TREES

Now prepare the trees by removing any dead branches and removing the lower branches up to about one-third of the tree's height to create a trunk.

Lift each tree from its pot, shake off excess soil and untangle the roots. Trim off large, unneeded roots and excess length but always leave enough to support the tree in good health.

Mist the trees and their roots to ensure they do not dry out while you are working on them. Keep trees moist and covered until you are ready to use them. It is best to do this procedure during the cooler months, to reduce the risk of the trees drying out.

PLANTING THE TREES

For this stage, refer back to your composition sketch (see page 83). The illustrations below give an example planting composition.

As you place each tree, carefully use the wires to anchor it in position. It is very important that the trees are unable to move once positioned, as this can damage fine roots.

Begin by selecting the two or three largest trees for your planting and position them as shown. The largest (primary tree) should be off center and nearer the front of the tray.

Working your way down the sizes, choose the next batch of trees and position accordingly. The direction of the group arrangement will now begin to form, based on the height and trunk thickness of the primary trees.

Finally, take your remaining trees (amongst the smallest), and position them mainly toward the side and rear of the planting. This will give the effect of depth and perspective to your group.

Use the soil mixture to fill the pot, covering all the roots. Water thoroughly.

FINISHING TOUCHES

To provide a natural, finished effect to the planting, you may choose to place some moss and/or some small shallow rocks on the soil surface. It may also be necessary to trim some of the lower branches of the more centrally placed trees so that the branches of one tree do not overlap with those of other trees.

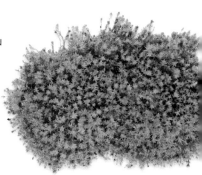

When repotting the group planting into its new pot in two or three years' time, the roots of all the trees should have fused together and the anchoring wires and frame can be cut out.

Chapter 3

SPECIES PROFILES

Here, we take a closer look at the tree species most often used for creating bonsai. Each tree species has specific requirements for its cultivation, training, and care. Knowledge about different species of bonsai is crucial to taking proper care of your tree. Knowing more about the species can also help you to select a good specimen in the first place.

We have only mentioned pests and diseases in this chapter where there are species-specific problems. Otherwise, please refer to the general pests and diseases section (pages 73–75).

ACER (MAPLE)

The Japanese Maple (*Acer palmatum*) comes originally from Japan, China, and Korea. The leaves resemble a hand with, in most cases, five pointed lobes—"Palma" being the Latin for "palm of hand." The bark of younger trees is normally green or reddish-green and turns light gray or grayish-brown as it ages. The new shoots in spring can be yellow, orange, or even bright red, and their red fall foliage is very attractive. They are extremely popular as bonsai and are imported in vast numbers from Japan. Other maples also used for bonsai may have only three lobes and less vivid fall colors (see Acer to Try below).

Choose your maple with care. Avoid specimens with ugly pruning scars and groups of branches emerging from the same point. These look unnatural and unsightly, and take a lot of time and work to correct.

GROWING AND CARE

Japanese maples prefer a sunny, airy position, but need some shade on very hot days. They are frost hardy, but should be protected from heavy frost and intense long-term freezing.

Water maples regularly throughout the growing season. When they have dropped their leaves, this can be reduced to a bare minimum as they are not photosynthesizing.

Repot every two years, using a well-drained soil mixture. Prune the roots thoroughly—the pot will fill with roots quite quickly.

Wire only when in leaf, as twigs with less sap in them in winter are very prone to snapping.

Shoots and twigs can be trimmed year round. Regularly cut new growth back to one or two pairs of leaves on each twig. Prune strong branches only in fall to prevent bleeding. Apply cut paste to the wounds, as Japanese maples are prone to fungal infections.

Feed every other week throughout the growing season.

Maples are subject to aphid infestation, so treat regularly with an insecticide.

ACER TO TRY
- *Acer buergerianum* (Trident maple)
- *Acer palmatum* 'Shindeshojo'
- *Acer palmatum* 'Kiyohime'
- *Acer palmatum* 'Seigen'
- *Acer campestre* (Field maple)

Acer palmatum 'Shindeshojo' is famous for its intense color changes.

Position boxwood in sun or partial shade and do not allow it to dry out.

BUXUS (BOXWOOD)

Originating from Europe, *Buxus* are densely branched shrubs. Most are hardy, although some can survive indoors. It is popular for bonsai as it has small leaves and a very fine branch structure. Two peculiarities—its wood is heavier than water so does not float and its leaves are poisonous. Boxwood has a naturally multi-stemmed growth pattern that lends itself to being styled like large spreading trees. They have dark-green leaves and shallow, fibrous root systems that often produce powerful surface roots and nebari (see page 22).

Boxwood are fast growers but are very slow to thicken. It is said that field-grown boxwood can have a trunk diameter as little as 3in after 20 or 30 years. The wood is hard and responds well to carving.

GROWING AND CARE

Position boxwood in sun or partial shade and protect from the worst of the weather during winter.

Keep the soil evenly moist and do not allow it to dry out, especially in windy or sunny weather.

Repot every two years in early spring.

Wiring should only be used for initial training; trimming and pruning is sufficient thereafter. Thin out inner foliage to allow light in.

Regular pruning in late spring helps to increase ramification; follow pruning with strict pinching for the rest of the year to refine the foliage. If you remove all the green foliage on a branch, that branch will be likely to die.

Feed weekly during summer months, using a general fertilizer.

Pests are not a big problem, but watch out for aphids and scale insects—use insecticide when needed.

BUXUS TO TRY

- *Buxus microphylla* 'Morris Midget'
- *Buxus sempervirens* (European box)
- *Buxus harlandii* (Harland box)

CARPINUS (HORNBEAM)

Hornbeams, a deciduous species, are distributed throughout temperate regions. The American hornbeam is an important native species within the eastern US; the European and Korean hornbeams are very closely related. The leaves are deep green and shiny, with toothed edges; prominent veins give them a corrugated appearance. They are a bronze color in spring; in fall they turn a blazing orange-yellow, sometimes with interesting, clearly defined splashes of red. Leaves are arranged alternately; the European species has ovate, wavy-edged leaves up to 4in, pale green in spring, appearing as late as May in the US, turning glossy green in summer then yellow to orange-brown in fall.

GROWING AND CARE

Place your hornbeam in a bright spot but not with too much direct sunlight. Protect it from severe freezing temperatures in winter.

Keep your trees moist, though not wet. Check regularly in summer.

Repot every two years in early spring, just before the tree starts growing.

Wiring needs to be carried out with great care as the bark marks easily and wire marks can take a long time to disappear, especially after spring growth. Try to make use of guy wires to move branches into shape if possible.

Wait for the new spring growth to harden off and then prune heavily to force the tree to grow new buds closer to the trunk. This creates better ramification.

Feed with a general fertilizer when the first growth appears and once every two weeks throughout spring and summer.

Very resistant to pests, but check from time to time for aphids—no plant is truly immune.

CARPINUS TO TRY

- *Carpinus betulus* (European hornbeam)
- *Carpinus turczaninowii* (Turczaninow hornbeam)

Carpinus caroliniana (American hornbeam) prefers a bright spot but not too much direct sunlight.

Cedrus atlantica Glauca Group (Atlas Cedar). Cedars prefer slightly dry conditions.

CEDRUS (CEDAR)

Some varieties of the *Cedrus* genus make excellent bonsai. Their rough, cragged bark is a feature of the species. The short needle clusters growing along the branches give them a unique canopy. A beautiful coniferous tree, but not frequently used as bonsai. The cedar's beauty is both unique and rare. If you can get your hands on one, you'll find them easy to grow and an enjoyable challenge to style and shape. There are four distinct cultivars suitable but only one commonly used, namely *Cedrus atlantica* Glauca Group (Atlas Cedar), which is much prized and easy to work.

GROWING AND CARE

The cedar likes sun and lots of it. Protect the tree from freezing temperatures in winter. Cedars do not like cold, drying winds.

Be careful not to overwater; cedars prefer slightly dry conditions. Make sure the soil mixture provides good drainage. Constantly moist soil will make the cedar bonsai's roots turn mushy and the needles turn yellow. But also take care not to allow the soil to dry out completely. Dry soil weakens the plant and may cause it to drop its needles.

Repot every two to four years, without disturbing the root system too much. Cedars have a tight root system, easily damaged. After repotting, keep the cedar bonsai out of the wind.

The branches of this slow-growing tree must remain wired for 12–24 months.

Once basic training is completed and the branches set in position, the tree needs little more than trimming of unwanted extensions.

Feed with a general fertilizer every two weeks throughout the growing season.

Cedar is not susceptible to pests or disease but it is wise to keep a watch for needle loss; if this occurs, treat for vine weevils and, if necessary, check the root system.

CEDRUS TO TRY

- *Cedrus atlantica* Glauca Group (Atlas Cedar)
- *Cedrus libani* (cedar of Lebanon)
- *Cedrus brevifolia* (Cyprus cedar)
- *Cedrus deodara* (Himalayan cedar)

CHAMAECYPARIS **(FALSE CYPRESS)**

Chamaecyparis is a popular genus for bonsai; they are slow-growing, evergreen coniferous trees from the forests of Taiwan, Japan, and North America. They have flat, overlapping sprays of scale-like adult leaves $\frac{1}{16}$–$\frac{3}{16}$in long. Their popularity as an ornamental garden plant, frequently used in rockeries, has led to large numbers of readily available varieties; the two species suitable for bonsai are *Chamaecyparis obtusa* (Hinoki cypress) and *Chamaecyparis pisifera* (Sawara cypress). They are easy to keep alive; however, they are not easy to style and maintain.

GROWING AND CARE

False cypresses are happiest in full sun but must be protected from strong wind, particularly during the winter.

Spray-mist the foliage regularly; they do not tolerate the soil drying out. Unlike many coniferous species, false cypresses are thirsty trees.

Repot every two to three years in standard soil mix as growth starts in early spring; they do not mind having their roots cut back.

Trimming is preferable to wiring when shaping the tree.

False cypresses need to be constantly pruned to allow light into the deeper reaches of the tree, otherwise dieback occurs and there will be no regrowth; this can be a major bonsai problem.

Keep trimmed with the "cut and grow" approach, rather more like topiary, with constant pinching of new foliage.

Feed with a general fertilizer every other week from spring to fall.

False cypresses are not seriously prone to disease but watch for aphids, red spider mites, and scale insects.

CHAMAECYPARIS TO TRY
- *Chamaecyparis obtusa* 'Nana Gracilis' (dwarf variety of Hinoki cypress)
- *Chamaecyparis pisifera* 'Boulevard' (Sawara cypress)
- *Chamaecyparis obtusa* 'Yatsubusa'
- *Chamaecyparis pisifera* 'Plumosa'

Chamaecyparis obtusa 'Nana Gracilis' is a dwarf variety of the Hinoki cypress.

CRATAEGUS (HAWTHORN)

The hawthorn is a shrub-like plant that takes many years to develop into an acceptable bonsai. For bonsai it has good characteristics: small leaves and white flowers followed by red berries. It is quite easy to grow but unfortunately it is not easy to dig up; many hawthorns die after being collected. It is a spiny, deciduous plant from the northern temperate regions of the world. Many hawthorns have irregular, almost muscular trunks with complex patterns of ridging; the bark is dark brown and has a tendency to peel off in large pieces.

GROWING AND CARE

Most hawthorns enjoy sun, with partial shade in the hottest part of midsummer; they dislike extreme heat but are resistant to windy conditions.

Water generously—do not allow the soil to dry out completely.

Repot every one to two years in early spring or fall. Always leave a strong root system. Up to a third of the root mass may be removed if necessary.

Wire during spring and summer where required and check regularly that the wires do not cut in as scars can be slow to heal.

Prune back shoots to the first two leaves on each twig. Hawthorn grows quickly and needs constant pruning.

Feed with a general fertilizer every two to three weeks from spring to fall.

Hawthorns can be susceptible to aphids, powdery mildew, rust, and leaf blight, so use both spray pesticide and fungicide regularly and keep in an area with good air circulation.

CRATAEGUS TO TRY

- *Crataegus cuneata* (Japanese hawthorn)
- *Crataegus monogyna* (common hawthorn, white or red)
- *Crataegus monogyna* 'Variegata' (mottled creamy-white leaves)

Crataegus is a spiny, deciduous plant from the northern temperate regions of the world.

FAGUS (BEECH)

Fagus is a genus of deciduous trees in the Fagaceae family, native to temperate regions of Europe, Asia, and North America. A large tree capable of reaching a great height, beech is undemanding and will survive most conditions. It does best in well-drained soils in areas of high humidity and can cope with little sunlight. *Fagus sylvatica*, the European beech, tolerates shallow chalk and clay soils; 'Atropunicea' is a pretty variation. *Fagus grandifolia*, the American Beech, is more commonly seen growing wild in the US. Japanese beech, *Fagus crenata*, is very closely related. If grown as solitary specimen trees, both European and Japanese species mature into tall stately trees with a spherical crown and branches that reach down to the ground. The bark is silvery in the Japanese species; the bark remains smooth even on very old specimens of both species.

European beech is an excellent species for bonsai cultivation, as it is hardy and tolerant of a wide range of conditions. Given time, the tree makes fine dense twigging and an excellent winter silhouette; many trees keep their brown leaves throughout the winter.

GROWING AND CARE

Beech trees will grow happily in semi-shade or full sun, but they do need to be sheltered from strong midday summer sun and from strong winds, both of which can cause leaves to scorch and brown.

Keep your tree moist, but not too wet.

Repot every two years or, in the case of very mature trees, four years in spring as the buds extend, using the standard soil mix. Older specimens can be repotted as and when it is obviously necessary.

Wiring is largely a design operation; new growth conforms, so trimming is the major care needed for training. Beech bark is extremely thin and scars easily, so do not leave any wire on for too long.

Most beech bonsai produce just one flush of growth each year, during May and June. Wait for the new spring growth to harden off and then prune heavily to force the tree to grow new buds closer to the trunk—you will then have a neater, more compact tree.

Feed with a general fertilizer when the first leaves start to unfurl and once every two weeks in late spring/summer.

Pests are not a significant problem but watch for mildew on the leaves if in a poorly ventilated area; treat with a fungicide if it occurs.

FAGUS TO TRY
- *Fagus sylvatica* (European beech)
- *Fagus crenata* (Japanese beech)

Fagus sylvatica (European beech) can tolerate shallow chalk and clay soils.

FICUS (FIG)

Figs are common to tropical and subtropical regions and are mistakenly called "indoor bonsai." They are only "indoor" in cool to cold regions where we experience frosts. Typical of all fig tree species is their milky latex sap, which will leak from wounds or cuts. Figs are evergreen with quite thick, pointed leaves and smooth gray bark. Most figs produce aerial roots growing downward from the branches.

GROWING AND CARE

Ficus are indoor bonsai in the winter months—they cannot endure frost—but they can be kept outside in summer, although they need to be in full sun. The temperature should be kept relatively constant. *Ficus* can endure low humidity due to their thick, waxy leaves, but they prefer a higher humidity.

Water regularly and generously whenever the soil gets slightly dry. Daily misting to maintain humidity is recommended; do not overdo this or fungal problems may appear. The warmer the position of the fig during winter, the more water it needs. If it overwinters in a cooler place, it only needs to be kept slightly moist.

Repot the tree every other year during spring, using a basic soil mixture.

Regular pruning retains the tree's shape. If you want the trunk to thicken, let the tree grow freely for one or two years. Cover larger wounds with a sealant to avoid losing sap.

Feed with a general fertilizer weekly or every two weeks, depending on the age of the tree—young, rapidly growing trees need feeding more frequently during summer.

FICUS TO TRY

- *Ficus benjamina* (weeping fig)
- *Ficus retusa* 'brevifolia'

Ficus bonsai cannot endure frost and should be kept indoors during winter.

JUNIPERUS (JUNIPER)

Junipers are evergreen coniferous trees or shrubs. Colors range from dark blue-greens to light greens and the foliage can be either scale-like or needle-like. They are very popular as bonsai and make some of the most beautiful bonsai you can possibly have. Junipers are very tough plants, but there are a couple of things to watch out for: spider mite infestations (which can take hold unnoticed) and overwatering. They are mountain shrubs that will survive with little water.

GROWING AND CARE

Place the tree outside, year-round, in a bright spot with lots of sunlight; protect from frost below 14°F.

Many people overwater junipers. Just ensure they are damp, not wet.

Repot every two years, using a basic, well-draining soil mix; very old trees can have even longer intervals.

The foliage pads should be wired and fanned out after thinning to let in light and air. Without this, the inner parts of the foliage pads will die.

Trim long shoots that stick out from the silhouette with sharp scissors throughout the growing season.

Use normal organic fertilizer pellets or granules every month during the growing season.

Use systemic bug sprays regularly to prevent spider mites from gaining a home (see page 74).

JUNIPERUS TO TRY
• *Juniperus chinensis* (Chinese juniper)
• *Juniperus sargentii* (Japanese Shimpaku)
• *Juniperus rigida* (needle juniper)

Two European species:
• *Juniperus sabina* (savin)
• *Juniperus communis* (common juniper)

Juniperus sargentii (Japanese Shimpaku) is a mountain shrub that will survive with little water.

LARIX (LARCH)

The larch is an unusual species, one of the small number of deciduous conifers; they bear bright green to bluish-green needle-like leaves that turn yellow in fall. The larch is a popular bonsai species as raw material with a thick trunk is relatively easy to obtain and it grows extremely fast in the early years, although the European larch, *Larix decidua*, slows as it matures. The Japanese larch, *Larix kaempferi*, is frequently used in plantation growing. The small cones that appear in spring usually start off purple in color before going brown and remain on the tree for a number of years before dropping. The larch has grayish bark that forms cracks and ridges in older specimens.

GROWING AND CARE

The larch grows well in full sun, preferably with some shade on the hottest days in summer to prevent scorching of the needles. Keep the tree outside year round, as it is extremely hardy and is happy in temperatures down to -4°F.

Keep evenly moist. Larches kept in full sun during summer can become very thirsty.

Repot annually in spring as the buds extend. Larch generally resents root disturbance, however; do not bare-root and do not root-prune heavily.

Larch is best wired in spring when the leaf buds are sprouting and the bare branches can still be seen; take care not to knock off new buds. If wire is left on over winter, the tree can be less hardy as the wire becomes very cold and damages the branches.

Larch is a strong tree that can withstand regular pruning.

Larches do well with a high-nitrogen feed in early spring, applied just before the buds start growing. In summer, switch to a balanced feed to help the larch harden off for the winter.

Larch is not seriously prone to infestation but check for aphids and scale insects.

LARIX TO TRY

- *Larix decidua* (European larch)
- *Larix kaempferi* (Japanese larch)

Larch is a strong tree that can withstand regular pruning.

LONICERA (HONEYSUCKLE)

Lonicera is a genus of about 108 species, of which many are climbers unsuitable for bonsai use. However, there are a number of shrubby loniceras that make excellent subjects for bonsai. The smaller, shrubbier honeysuckles are evergreen and frequently used for hedging. Their leaves are small and they grow well even from old wood. The larger-leaved, flowering loniceras are deciduous and produce highly colored, sweet-smelling flowers; they are climbers, often growing rapidly, and are much more difficult to control. Trunks tend to be stiff, erect, and difficult to bend; content yourself with straight-trunked styles.

GROWING AND CARE

Place in full sun. If the temperature drops below 23°F you will lose leaves even with evergreen varieties, but they will soon be replaced in the spring.

Keep well watered in the growing season. If you have small specimens in small pots, protect from severe frosts as freezing prevents water being taken in by the roots and dehydration may occur.

Repot in spring as new leaf buds appear. Use standard bonsai soil mix; honeysuckles will survive in most soils as long as they do not become waterlogged.

The branches are brittle and do not respond well to wiring.

Constant clipping is essential to keep foliage pads tidy and to encourage dense growth. Foliage should be thinned out in the spring to allow light to reach inner leaves. Carving or hard pruning can be carried out during late fall and winter.

Feed with general fertilizer every two weeks throughout the growing season.

Honeysuckles are not susceptible to any particular pest infestation but leaves may become mildewed if there is not good air circulation.

LONICERA TO TRY

- *Lonicera nitida* (small green-leafed species)
- *Lonicera nitida* 'Baggesen's gold' (similar, but with a yellow tinge to the leaves)
- *Lonicera pileata* (box-leaved honeysuckle; slightly larger leaves)

Flowering *lonicera* are deciduous and produce highly colored, sweet-smelling flowers.

MALUS (CRAB APPLE)

The *Malus* genus consists of around 35 varieties of deciduous trees, found in Europe and Asia. The crab apple is one of the most popular flowering species in bonsai cultivation, with flowers in spring and beautiful little apples in fall. Flowers vary considerably from white, through creamy-white to pink, while fruit range from tiny to marble-sized and are colored purple, red, orange, or yellow. *Malus cerasifera* (Nagasaki crab apple) is the most commonly grown as bonsai due to its prolific white flowers, which are pink in bud with red fruit. *Malus sylvestris* (European crab apple) has leaves up to 2in long, pink-flushed white flowers in late spring, and yellow or red-flushed fruit, while *Malus halliana* (Hall crab apple) has pink flowers, glossy green foliage, and purple fruits, which can be sparse.

GROWING AND CARE

Malus require plenty of sunlight; place the tree outside in full sun. The tree is hardy and needs little protection from freezing temperatures. Provide good air circulation to discourage mildew problems.

Water well when the tree is fruiting, making sure the tree does not dry out at this time; if it does, the fruits will shrivel and drop.

Repot annually in early spring, before the first signs of growth.

Wire new growth when it is long enough to place wire on; this could take a whole season for new shoots.

Prune in the spring on new shoots, reducing to one or two leaves. Leave unpruned until late summer, otherwise the tree is more likely to produce leaves than flower buds the following year. If fruit is not required, dead-head the flowers.

Feed with a high-potassium feed every other week in late summer until flower buds for next year are established, around late fall. Feeding after flowering can cause leaf growth at the expense of fruiting. If vigorous growth is required at the expense of fruit, continue to feed every other week, otherwise cease feeding until the fruits are well developed. To protect the vigor of the tree, it is better to allow the tree to fruit only every two or three years, as fruiting weakens the tree.

Crab apples attract many insects and diseases, particularly aphids, red spider mites, caterpillars, apple scab, and mildew, so spray regularly with both insecticides and fungicides (see pages 73–75).

MALUS TO TRY

- *Malus sylvestris* (European crab apple)
- *Malus halliana* (Hall crab apple)
- *Malus cerasifera* (Nagasaki crab apple)

Malus halliana (Hall crab apple) has beautiful pink flowers when in bloom.

OLEA (OLIVE)

A native of the Mediterranean, the olive is an evergreen tree growing to about 30ft and cultivated for its rich fruit and oils. The olive has deep-green leaves with grayish undersides, and produces yellowish-white flowers followed by green or black fruit in late summer or early fall. It is much loved by bonsai enthusiasts for its rich historical and mythical lore as well as its elegant shiny leaves and its trunk, which takes on an aged, stony appearance when old; the olive will live for hundreds of years. *Olea europaea* is one of over 20 cultivars and the one most commonly kept as bonsai. Thought for some years to be an indoor tree, this has now been proved to be a myth; they are hardy down to 32°F and below, but less willing to produce fruit in lower temperatures.

GROWING AND CARE

Place the olive bonsai outside in a sunny spot; this also helps to reduce the size of the leaves.

Water well in summer but keep almost dry in winter and protect from frost—if the soil is wet and gets frozen, the roots will freeze and then rot.

Repot every two to three years in spring, as the buds sprout. Trim about one-third of the root ball, and remove a proportional number of the old leaves.

Wire young branches between fall and spring. Olive branches bruise easily so check frequently that the wire is not cutting in.

If pruning is done in spring, the resultant growth around the cut can be vigorous. The best time to prune is in late summer. In young trees, prune smaller shoots back to the last two or three leaves. Shoot-pruning and pinching encourages smaller leaves. Do not prune if the temperature falls below 50°F.

Feed with a general fertilizer every two weeks in the growing season but do not feed for three months after repotting.

OLEA TO TRY

• *Olea europaea* and its varieties 'Arbequina', 'Cipressino', 'El Greco', 'Frantoio', 'Hojiblanca', and 'Manzanilla'. Ask the advice of a specialist when you come to buy your plant to make sure the olive you intend to grow as bonsai outside will cope with your climate.

If you intend to grow your olive bonsai outside, be sure to select a variety that will cope with your climate.

PINUS (PINE)

Pines are considered to be at the top of the bonsai prestige ladder, with some classic specimens many hundreds of years old still existing in Japan. They are not always easy and have very specific needs but are very rewarding and make amazing bonsai specimens. Pines are evergreen and have an excellent appearance, even in winter. The individual needles do not persist forever, but each species retains its needles for up to three or more years. Old needles are shed in late fall and, to some extent, in spring. New needles are produced in spring. During this process, the tree is never without a "full complement" of needles.

GROWING AND CARE

There are four main species used for bonsai and they have very specific and slightly different requirements for healthy growth. If you do not adhere to these rules, you could adversely affect the health of your pines.

- *Pinus sylvestris* (Scots pine) and *Pinus mugo* (mountain pine) are European species, able to withstand very harsh conditions. Both are two-needle varieties and can happily live outside even in severe weather as well as in hot, sunny conditions. For maximum health and vigor, feed mountain and Scots pines regularly, ensuring that slow-release fertilizer is on the soil surface during the growing season through to late summer.

- *Pinus thunbergii* (Japanese black pine) trees are very hardy but only when in the poor soil typical of a Japanese mountainside. If the soil is rich and moist, they must be given winter protection. If the roots are wet and they freeze, they will rot. Again, this is a two-needle variety, but of greater length than the European pines.

- *Pinus parviflora* (Japanese white pine) trees are frequently grafted onto black pine rootstock; this makes them hardier and easier to care for. This is the only true five-needle pine suitable for bonsai. Provide a sunny position and protect from too much water in winter; they do not need temperature protection but they must be kept where you can control their level of moisture.

Pinus parviflora
(Japanese white pine)
is the only true
five-needle pine
suitable for bonsai.

GROWING AND CARE FOR ALL PINES, NOT CULTIVAR SPECIFIC

Repot all pines every two to three years; start repotting later than other trees, when it is quite obvious from the buds that the new season's growth has started, just before the buds begin to swell and extend. Be sure to use a well-drained soil mixture containing at least 30 per cent grit.

Pruning and trimming can become very complicated but if you stick to the basic rules you will produce good results. As the buds emerge at the start of the growing season, pinch out any more than two buds on any one branch or twig—if you do not do this, you will have a cartwheel of new branches all coming from the same point. When the new buds appear, allow them to grow until they are at least 1¼in in length. Take sharp-pointed scissors and cut back to half the length, pointing the scissors downward to avoid cutting through the newly emerging needles.

Use a general fertilizer on a monthly basis to keep the tree healthy. Stop feeding at the end of August.

PINUS TO TRY

- *Pinus sylvestris* (Scots pine)
- *Pinus mugo* (mountain pine)
- *Pinus thunbergii* (Japanese black pine)
- *Pinus parviflora* (Japanese white pine)
- *Pinus sylvestris* 'Beuvronensis' and *P. sylvestris* 'Watereri'
- *Pinus densiflora*
- *Pinus thunbergii* 'Corticosa'

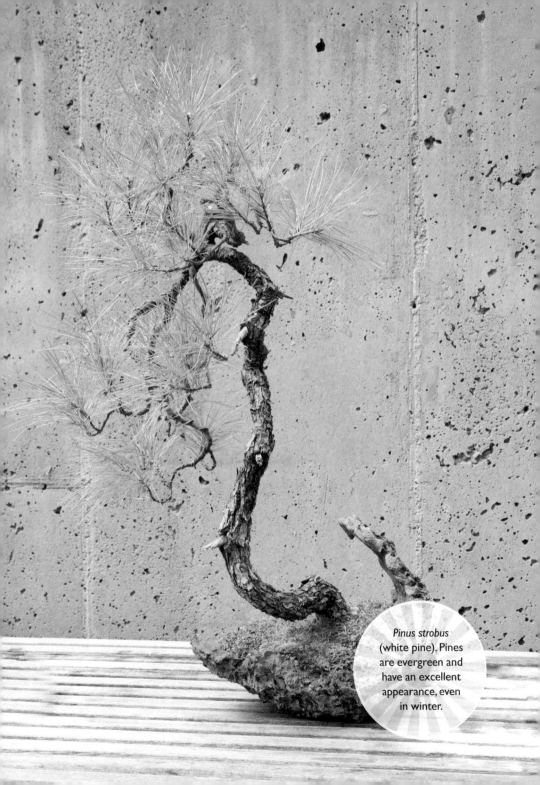

Pinus strobus (white pine). Pines are evergreen and have an excellent appearance, even in winter.

PRUNUS (STONE FRUIT)

This genus of over 300 flowering and fruiting trees is not covered by just one English species name. It covers, in fact, a whole group of deciduous or evergreen trees and shrubs, widely distributed throughout northern temperate regions and South America to Southeast Asia. The *Prunus* genus consists of apricot, cherry, peach, blackthorn, and plum, to mention but a few. All are suitable for development as bonsai, some for their flowers, some for the fruit, and others for their remarkable trunk coloring and markings; all respond well to bonsai training and are not difficult to maintain. Two points to consider: flowering trees are quite spectacular but only for a very short period; also, fruit does not reduce in size as the trees develop as bonsai, so choose naturally small-fruited varieties.

GROWING AND CARE

Prunus are happy with full sun or partial shade and some winter protection to avoid loss of next season's buds; you will not lose the tree, just the flowers.

Water regularly when required, do not let the trees dry out.

Repot annually in late winter, before the buds start to open.

Prune back hard after the flowers have dropped; if you want the fruit to set, delay pruning flowering branches until fall. Do not prune *Prunus* when they are dormant (without leaves) as it is known to increase the risk of silver leaf infection.

Feed using a general fertilizer every two weeks throughout the summer to ensure buds for the next year's flowers.

Prunus trees are susceptible to infestation from aphids, caterpillars, and birds, which enjoy the flower buds. Diseases include peach leaf curl, silver leaf, and blossom wilt. Treat every other week with systemic insecticide and fungicide throughout the season.

PRUNUS TO TRY

- *Prunus mume* (Japanese apricot)
- *Prunus spinosa* (blackthorn)
- *Prunus incisa* (Fuji cherry)
- *Prunus persica* (peach)
- *Prunus salicina* (Japanese plum)
- *Prunus serrulata* (flowering cherry)

Prunus cerasifera (cherry plum) flowering trees are quite spectacular but only for a very short period.

PYRACANTHA (FIRETHORN)

Pyracantha is a genus of about seven species of spiny evergreen shrubs with a spreading-to-erect habit. Native through southern Europe to Southwest Asia, the Himalayas, China, and Taiwan, mature specimens can reach heights of around 13–16ft. They are commonly cultivated in the US to grow up walls and other places where green coverage is needed. They are eminently suitable to grow as bonsai but be aware that they are called "firethorn" because their spines can cause inflammation and discomfort. They are cherished for their year-round foliage, abundant flowering capabilities, and spectacular fall and winter display of red or orange berries. *Pyracantha angustifolia* ("narrow leaf") is native to China and hardy to 28°F when grown in a bonsai container. *Pyracantha coccinea*, (scarlet firethorn), native to south-east Europe, is similar but more frost hardy. There are a large number of varieties with different berry colors.

GROWING AND CARE

Pyracanthas are able to withstand dry and drought conditions. Position in full sun and in a well-ventilated position to discourage fungal diseases.

Pyracantha prefers moist soil so needs moderate watering, but do not let the pot dry out.

Repot every year in spring, using a well-drained soil to ensure waterlogging does not occur.

Prune hard in late winter or early spring. Pinch out new growth throughout the growing season and remove fading berries.

Feed every other week with a high-nitrogen feed from early spring to early summer, then switch to a low-nitrogen feed for the remainder of the growing season, especially if you have had a good crop of berries.

The most serious threat to the health of a *Pyracantha* bonsai is fireblight, a fungal disease spread by leaf hopper insects. Unfortunately, once infected there is no way to cure your plant. You can, however, take steps to protect your tree. First, watch carefully for any insect activity in or around the plant. If you spot any insects, remove them immediately. Second, reduce or eliminate your plant's exposure to other bonsai, especially other *Pyracantha* trees. Third, always be sure to wash your hands before and after handling your plant.

PYRACANTHA TO TRY

- *Pyracantha angustifolia* ("narrow leaf")
- *Pyracantha coccinea* (scarlet firethorn)

Pyracanthas are called "firethorn" because their spines can cause inflammation and discomfort.

QUERCUS (OAK)

Quercus species are strong and hardy trees, very suitable for bonsai purposes. There are more than 600 species within this genus; both deciduous and evergreen oaks have spirally arranged leaves, with lobate margins in most cultivars. They are found in many regions in the northern hemisphere, all bearing fruit called acorns. Acorns are not produced until the tree is at least 40 years old. English oaks are arguably the best known and loved of British native trees; they are slow-growing, long-lived and deciduous. *Quercus petraea* (sessile oak) closely resembles *Quercus robur* (English oak) but has longer leaves. *Quercus cerris* (Turkey oak) is a tough, fast-growing deciduous tree with gray-white bark, while *Quercus ilex* (holm oak), from southern Europe, is more tender and has spiny evergreen leaves.

GROWING AND CARE

Place in partial shade or full sun; oaks are hardy, but should be protected if temperatures drop very low in the winter.

The oak has no particular watering needs but make sure the soil never dries out completely.

Repot every two years, just before the tree starts to grow in early spring.

You can be quite severe with pruning and trimming without impairing growth; oaks usually respond well with strong growth. However, they are slow to develop so you may wait many years before you have thick-trunked mature bonsai.

Feed with a general fertilizer every two or three weeks during the growing season.

QUERCUS TO TRY
- *Quercus robur* (English oak)
- *Quercus petraea* (sessile oak)
- *Quercus cerris* (Turkey oak)
- *Quercus ilex* (holm oak)

Quercus robur (English oak) are slow-growing, long-lived, and deciduous.

RHODODENDRON (AZALEA)

Azaleas originally from Asia are evergreen, while the North American varieties are deciduous; they form part of the genus *Rhododendron*, with small, quite spectacular flowers, which open in May to June and come in many different colors, shapes, and sizes. They are extremely popular bonsai because of the quantity and variety of the flowers. Remember, all rhododendron varieties are "lime-haters" so use ericaceous lime-free feed and soil mix.

GROWING AND CARE

Azaleas thrive in sunny spots, but provide them with some shade.

When flowering, azaleas should be protected from rain to make the flowers last longer. Healthy, mature azaleas can endure some frost but should be protected from temperatures lower than 23°F.

Azaleas should not be allowed to dry out but do not like permanently wet roots. Check the moisture of the soil carefully.

Repot once every two years, either in spring or after flowering. Prune the roots with care because they are thin, tightly matted, and can be easily torn when disentangling.

The wood of azaleas is brittle; wiring and bending should be done with great care.

Prune immediately after flowering—wilted flowers should be removed. This is a good time to prune, because in summer next year's flower buds will develop and you do not want to cut those off. Unwanted shoots from the trunk or base of the branches can be removed at any time.

Feed regularly throughout the growing season using an ericaceous feed; these are lime-hating trees and the use of speciality feed is preferable. Use of other feeds may cause yellowing of leaves.

Treat with pesticide when required.

RHODODENDRON TO TRY

- *Rhododendron kiusianum*
- *Rhododendron kaempferi*
- *Rhododendron obtusum*
- The following varieties of *Rhododendron indicum*: 'Satsuki', 'Chinzan', 'Hakurei', 'Kaho', 'Kazan', and 'Kinsai'.

Rhododendron indicum 'Satsuki'. When flowering, azaleas should be protected from rain to make the flowers last longer.

TAXUS (YEW)

A key feature of the yew is its peeling reddish bark, making the tree look old, a quality highly appreciated for bonsai trees. Yew is a slow-growing evergreen tree with a slim and elegantly shaped trunk. The seeds and leaves are poisonous. The most common species are *Taxus baccata*, the English yew, and *Taxus cuspidata*, the Japanese yew, which has darker green leaves than the English yew, with light green undersides. This species has historical associations dating back to medieval times and the wood was an essential resource in the creation of the longbows that were used as weapons, as well as spears. They make excellent bonsai as they are easy to carve and have year-round interest with their dark green foliage.

GROWING AND CARE

Yews are flexible with regard to position and will tolerate full sun or partial shade; however, their large fleshy roots are vulnerable to frost damage when in bonsai pots.

Yews do not like to dry out totally but are prone to root rot if they sit in water; ensure that the soil is kept moist at all times, but not wet.

Repot every two to three years into a well-draining mix.

Yews respond well to pruning and easily develop foliage pads. They back-bud profusely on old and new wood and new branches are always readily available on the main trunk. However, if you like the yew to grow fruits, significant pruning must wait until fall—do not prune in the growing season. Cut new growth with scissors to encourage back-budding. Thinning out the foliage along the branches allows light to reach the branches, which stimulates new buds to grow and promotes back-budding.

Apply a general fertilizer every two to three weeks throughout the entire growing season.

TAXUS TO TRY
- *Taxus baccata* (English yew)
- *Taxus cuspidata* (Japanese yew)

Taxus cuspidata (Japanese yew) make excellent bonsai as they are easy to carve and have evergreen foliage.

ULMUS (ELM)

There are many species in the *Ulmus* genus, most of which have been almost completely decimated in the last 50 years by "Dutch elm disease," a fungal infection that has killed millions of trees in the US. The Chinese elm (*Ulmus parvifolia*) has so far been a resistant strain. Coming from Southeast Asia and having naturally very small leaves, it is a very good variety for bonsai training and easy to train for beginners. In many places they are sold as indoor bonsai, because they are very accommodating and can adapt to indoor conditions. However, they are truly frost-hardy trees that can withstand temperatures down to -13°F—very cold indeed. But do not put a tree outside in winter that has been living indoors—they must have a standard fall outside to acclimatize.

GROWING AND CARE

The Chinese elm grows well in full sun and partial shade. In most climates, they can stay outside during the winter. Depending on the temperature of their winter quarters, Chinese elms can either drop their leaves or keep them until spring, when the new shoots emerge.

Water generously as soon as the soil gets dry and avoid both drought and permanent wetness.

Repot young Chinese elms every two years; older and large specimens can be repotted at longer intervals. Spring is the best time for repotting. Root-pruning should be done with care as it tends to produce crooked and intertwined roots. Work on them very carefully in order to create a regular, good nebari.

The elm is a very accommodating and rewarding tree to work with. It can be shaped well with normal wiring and guy wires.

If you let a Chinese elm grow freely, it will thicken rapidly; they respond well to frequent trimming and produce dense ramification. They also bud well from old wood after strong pruning; allow shoots to extend to three or four nodes, then prune back to one or two leaves. Late fall is a good time for pruning.

Feed with general fertilizer well during the growing season.

ULMUS TO TRY
- *Ulmus parvifolia* (Chinese elm)
- *Ulmus procera* (English elm)

The elm is a very accommodating and rewarding tree to work with.

DISPLAYING YOUR BONSAI

Whether you have just one bonsai or a collection, with a little thought and planning it can become a real feature in your garden. Like any piece of art, bonsai needs to be shown off to its best. By choosing the correct positioning with sufficient light, sun, and shelter, bonsai will not just survive but thrive.

SITING YOUR BONSAI

Choose a site where you will get the maximum benefit and viewing pleasure. Think about which area of the garden is best to view from the house.

Ensure that the site will receive sufficient sunlight. All trees require light; however, some varieties of bonsai would not want to be located in too shady an area, especially evergreen species, as light intensity can affect the color of their foliage.

There needs to be enough protection from prevailing winds. Avoid any areas that would be affected by a wind tunnel created between nearby buildings, or low-lying shaded areas that could be a frost trap.

Make sure your bonsai are safely placed away from hazards such as footballs bouncing over the fence from children playing next door, and out of reach of pets and pests.

The spot chosen must be convenient for watering and routine maintenance. Somewhere close to an often-used path will provide a welcome opportunity for you to stop regularly as you pass. This helps you to observe progress closely, monitor plant health and spot any potential problems in good time.

Adequate thought must also be given to the security of your treasured possessions. Too many bonsai have been stolen because they are easily spotted by passers-by.

Most importantly, remember to add somewhere to sit down, relax, and enjoy views of your collection of bonsai.

A TASTE OF THE ORIENT

By simply planting a clump of bamboo or positioning a large maple in a pot close to your bonsai, you can evoke the Japanese heritage of bonsai. If you wish to include further Japanese elements to your garden, consider adding a water feature, some granite lanterns, stepping stones, clipped shrubs, or perhaps even a Zen garden, with large rocks and attractively raked gravel.

IDEAS FOR DISPLAY

Here are a few ideas for displaying your bonsai to get you started. Remember to display your trees at eye level, to get the most visual enjoyment out of them.

VERTICAL POLES OR PILLARS

Professional bonsai gardens often display their most important trees on poles (see photo, page 132). This puts them at eye level and makes them stand out. The most frequently used materials are old railway sleepers, old telegraph poles, or tree trunks. Other options are stone slabs or pillars made of concrete or bricks. Placing the pillars in front of a plain-colored fence will really make the trees stand out. They would also look great arranged around a pond.

BENCHES

A bench is the most straightforward method of displaying your trees, although it could start to look cluttered if your collection grows. The quality of the wood is important, as well as the regular use of preservatives.

TOKONOMA

This is a typically Japanese presentation—a tranquil spot (usually an alcove, though it could be simply a sheltered part of the garden) in which to admire your bonsai. The tokonoma and its contents are essential elements of traditional Japanese decoration, usually comprising a bonsai tree and a scroll and accent plant to accentuate the tree on display and

create a sense of harmony. A successful companion planting is beautiful in its own right, but should never become the dominant part of the tokonoma display. The accent plant should be positioned in such a way that the bonsai will be accentuated.

CHOOSING ACCENT PLANTS

The accent, or companion plant, can be a flowering plant, bamboo, grass, ferns, or a moss variety. Here are some factors to help determine the kind and size of accent plant that fits best with the design:

SEASON—The accent plant should resemble the current season. This means the color of leaves and the presence of fruits or flowers is of great importance and should relate to the tree at that time of year.

STYLE—Trees that represent a struggle to survive, like a windswept style or growing on a rock, should be accompanied by a not-too-luxuriant accent plant. Taller styles, like the literati, can be displayed with a tall grass variety. Lowland plants can be accompanied by mosses and ferns.

CONTRAST—Bonsai trees with flowers or fruits should be contrasted by non-flowering accent plants, and vice versa.

COMBINATIONS—When combining several plants to create an accent plant, make sure those selected come from similar origins.

GLOSSARY

ADVENTITIOUS BUD
A bud that occurs in an unusual place on a tree.

AIR-LAYERING
A technique used to force a tree or branch to form new roots at a certain point.

AKADAMA
A specialized fine gravel soil for growing bonsai trees.

APEX
The highest point of a tree; it can be a single branch or a number of small branches.

APICAL
Vigorous growth produced by a tree—generally at the top of the tree, furthest from the roots.

BACK-BUDDING
A technique used to encourage growth back along the branches by pruning the end growth.

BARK
The outermost layers of the trunk and branches of trees.

BLEED
To weep sap from a cut or wound.

BRANCHES
Primary branches grow directly from the trunk; secondary branches grow directly from the primary branches; tertiary branches grow directly from the secondary branches.

BROAD-LEAVED
Broad-leaved trees are a large group of plants which have seeds enclosed in an ovary. Also known as deciduous trees, these go dormant in fall until spring.

BUD
An organ or shoot containing an embryonic branch, leaf, or flower.

BUTTRESSING
The base of the tree flares outward giving the impression of age and solidity. Also known as "nebari," or root-flare.

CALLUS
Tissue that forms over a wound on a trunk as part of the healing process.

CAMBIUM
Green growth tissue directly below the bark.

CANDLE
The name given to the extending bud of a pine tree before the new needles open.

CONIFERS

Evergreen trees that typically bear cones and have needle-like leaves.

CULTIVAR

A cultivated variety of a given species.

DEADWOOD

A technique used to create unnatural deadwood on a bonsai which enhances the character and age-appearance of a tree.

DECIDUOUS

Broad-leaved trees that shed leaves in the fall and have a period of dormancy during the winter.

DEFOLIATION

A technique that involves the removal of all or most of the leaves, used to reduce the plant's leaf size as well as the distance between internodes. Not to be used unless the tree is growing well. This is an advanced procedure and should only be carried out on more mature bonsai by experienced growers.

DESICCATION

A state of serious dryness.

DIEBACK

The death of end growth, beginning at the tip due to disease or injury.

DISSECT

To deeply cut into segments or lobes.

ERICACEOUS

A term referring to acid-loving, lime-hating plants.

EVERGREEN

A plant that remains in leaf year round, slowly shedding old leaves and replacing them with new growth. This normally applies to conifers.

FOLIAGE PADS

A mass of foliage on a branch, sometimes referred to as a "cloud."

FORM

The main direction in which the trunk of a tree grows.

GENUS

A group of plants that belong to the same family of varying species.

GRAFT
A technique used to meld or attach a branch to the stump or trunk of a tree.

INDOOR BONSAI
A term used to describe tropical or sub-tropical plants that need to be kept inside in temperate climates where temperatures dip below 59°F.

INTERNODE
The section of growth between two nodes (leaves or leaf-joints).

JIN
The removal of bark on a branch to create deadwood.

NEBARI
Root mound, or flare; exposed root form.

OVERWATERING
Watering too much and too often, and in poorly drained soil; this can decrease the amount of air available to roots, leading to root-rot and the death of a tree.

PEN-JING (CHINESE)
Landscape planting.

PETIOLE
The stalk of a leaf that attaches to the stem.

PHLOEM
Specialized cells that transport the products of photosynthesis—e.g. sugars—from the leaves to all parts of the plant.

PHOTOSYNTHESIS
The plant's process of turning water and carbon dioxide into food using the energy from the sun.

POTENSAI
Potential bonsai.

PRE-BONSAI
A young tree that has not yet been trained.

PRUNING
An important method in training a bonsai by trimming leaves and/or branches.

RAMIFICATION
Repeated division of branches into secondary branches by means of pruning.

REPOTTING

The process of transferring a plant from one pot to another, usually a bigger pot, or to refresh the potting soil for a plant remaining in the same pot.

ROCK PLANTING

Trees grown in or on rocks to create a dramatic visual appearance.

ROOT OVER ROCK

A style of bonsai where the tree is planted over a rock with the roots extending downward to reach the soil.

SHARI

The technique used to create deadwood on a trunk.

SOIL

The medium for growing bonsai. Specialized soil for bonsai contains various mixtures of organic soil and inorganic soil containing stone, mineral or fired clay such as grit, sand, and Akadama.

SPECIES

The sub-division of a genus.

STYLE

The way in which a bonsai has been shaped in order to complement the form (direction) of the trunk.

TERMINAL BUD

A bud formed at the tip of a stem, twig, or branch.

TOKONOMA

Traditional Japanese display area in a home.

UNDER-WATERING

When a tree is allowed to dry out completely.

WIRING

A technique using wire to bend a branch or trunk in a certain direction, thus training it to grow in that direction.

XYLEM

Specialized cells used to transport water and nutrients required for photosynthesis from the roots to the leaves of the tree.

FURTHER RESOURCES

For more information on growing, training, and caring for bonsai, including specialist areas such as pests and diseases, as well as information on where to obtain the trees and equipment you may require, refer to the following:

PLANT SOCIETIES

Many of these national organizations have regional, and even city-by-city chapters. The best way to learn about bonsai is to make friends who enjoy it as well. You can look up the chapter closest to you. Monthly meetings generally include a guest speaker, plant swap, and preparations for upcoming shows.

American Bonsai Society
www.absbonsai.org

Mid America Bonsai Alliance
www.mababonsai.org

Bonsai Clubs International
www.bonsai-bci.com

PLACES TO VIEW BONSAI

Get inspired to create your own bonsai by visiting these public gardens and museums with extensive bonsai collections. Some of the trees are hundreds of years old, and most have been gifted to the gardens by private collectors.

New York Botanical Garden
www.nybg.org

The National Bonsai Museum
www.bonsai-nbf.org

Longwood Gardens
http://longwoodgardens.org

The Huntington
www.huntington.org

Pacific Bonsai Museum
http://pacificbonsaimuseum.org

Arnold Arboretum
www.arboretum.harvard.edu

BONSAI SUPPLIES AND MATERIALS

This is a selection of bonsai suppliers around the US. All online stores ship and some have physical locations. A few of the suppliers also offer plants, though you can also purchase these at your local garden center. If you're hoping to start small, online may well be the way to go, as many landscape specimens are already larger than a tabletop container.

Bonsai by Fields
www.bonsaibyfields.com

Brussel's Bonsai
http://brusselsbonsai.com

Dallas Bonsai
www.dallasbonsai.com

Dragon Tree Bonsai
www.dragontreebonsai.com

Golden Arrow Bonsai
www.goldenarrowbonsai.com

Hollow Creek Bonsai
www.hollowcreekbonsai.com

Mirai Bonsai
www.bonsaimirai.com

PUBLICATIONS

Many of the bonsai shops listed have bonsai-specific publications that cover pruning techniques in depth. Here is a selection of publications to help you learn more about plant selection and care for specific types of plants— particularly conifers and Japanese maples, two highly popular plants for bonsai.

Bonsai by Peter Warren (DK 2014)

Bonsai Today: Masters Series
A series of books, on subjects including pines, junipers, and shohin (Stone Lantern)

Bonsai with Japanese Maples by Peter Adams (Timber Press 2006)

Gardening with Conifers by Adrian Bloom (Firefly Books 2007)

International Bonsai Magazine
www.internationalbonsai.com

Japanese Maples: The Complete Guide to Selection and Cultivation by Peter Gregory and J. D. Vertrees (Timber Press 2010)

Niwaki: Pruning, Training and Shaping Trees the Japanese Way by Jake Hobson (Timber Press 2007)

Principles of Bonsai Tree Design by David De Groot (ABS Book Service)

Trees for All Seasons: Broadleaved Evergreens for Temperate Climates by Sean Hogan (Timber Press, 2008)

INDEX